P9-CAO-527

_to: Franceser_

# GLADYS,

## MY UNFORGETTABLE LOVE

ANTONIO E. MORALES-PITA PHD

_With best wishes,_

_Morales_

 FriesenPress

Suite 300 - 990 Fort St
Victoria, BC, V8V 3K2
Canada

www.friesenpress.com

Copyright © 2017 by Antonio E. Morales-Pita
First Edition — 2017

All rights reserved.

No part of this publication may be reproduced in any form, or by any means, electronic or mechanical, including photocopying, recording, or any information browsing, storage, or retrieval system, without permission in writing from FriesenPress.

ISBN
978-0-692-03338-8 (Hardcover)
978-0-692-80081-2 (Paperback)
978-1-5255-0219-4 (eBook)

1. BIOGRAPHY & AUTOBIOGRAPHY, PERSONAL MEMOIRS

Distributed to the trade by The Ingram Book Company

In memoriam to my wife, Gladys,
who made my life so much worth living
in such a complete way

# ACKNOWLEDGMENTS

My wife's cousin, Clarita, who, besides suggesting to me the idea of writing this book, contributed to improve it with her suggestions.

My niece, Marthica, who suggested to me the idea of writing this book

My spiritual father, Reverend Edgar Morales,

who helped Gladys and me to become better Christians.

# Table of Contents

ACKNOWLEDGMENTS                                              v

PROLOGUE                                                     ix

CHAPTER I -                                                  1
    HER LOYALTY AND SINCERITY

CHAPTER II -                                                 7
    GLADYS' INTERACTION WITH JEALOUSY

CHAPTER III -                                                15
    HER STRUGGLE TO IMPROVE HER MAN

CHAPTER IV -                                                 27
    HER FIRMNESS, BRAVERY, PRINCIPLES,
    AND VALUES

CHAPTER V -                                                  37
    HER EXTRAORDINARY HUMAN
    RELATIONS

CHAPTER VI -                                                 43
     HER LOVE AND IDENTIFICATION
     WITH CHILDREN

CHAPTER VII -                                            47
     THE DIVERSE WAYS OF EXPRESSING
     LOVE FOR HER MAN

CHAPTER VIII -                                        61
     HER EXEMPLARY MODESTY

CHAPTER IX -                                          67
     THE EXTRAORDINARY WAY IN
     WHICH SHE FACED DEATH

CHAPTER X -                                             75
     GLADYS MORALES' LEGACY

SURVEY                                                         79

REVIEWS                                                 81

# PROLOGUE

It is six o'clock in a prematurely cold autumn in Chicago. I have just entered my home accompanied by my friend Paul, who has helped me pick up Gladys' clothes and bring our oxygen compressor back home. Now I am alone with my thoughts. It is possible to be mentally prepared to survive painful moments and at the same time be confused. It is convenient and possible to take care of getting life and funeral insurance for two people and even to pay for cremation services in advance. Wills and powers of attorney can be legally and carefully prepared ahead of time. Written instructions can be delivered to the executor of our documents, including names and phone numbers of institutions to be called in moments of grief. It was not possible, though, to buy insurance that would cover the deep pain that would be experienced upon losing one of the members of the couple.

During the previous three weeks I had been getting used to the loneliness at home, in the living room, in my bed. I had witnessed her death in my arms, and she had expired under my kisses and love songs. Despite all these events, one did not accept reality. All of sudden, a surprise. Her phone was ringing, and during the last months, the phone calls only came from me. She had assigned herself a phone call reminder to take a medicine. Now she couldn't pick up the phone! I could not stop sobbing. She hadn't wanted me to cry and urged me to be happy, to get on with my life, to be an optimist, to fight to achieve my goals, and to be strong in her honor.

I walked to the east side of my apartment window, from which I could see Lake Michigan. A draft of fresh air slapped my face. This was a sign of early autumn in Chicago. I felt cold. It was October 6, 2015. I took a look at Sheridan Road between Hollywood and Ardmore, always jammed with traffic. Caressed the treadmill where Gladys exercised holding the oximeter in one of her fingers. Sat down on the bike, which she'd also used to check her oxygen level. I grabbed one of the photos where we were smiling together on our thirty-ninth anniversary, kissed it, and shed some tears. I entered the kitchen and could see her handwritten recipes for cooking black beans, white rice, baked fish, soups.

In those moments, my imagination flew to the past. I remembered my insistence on having her stop smoking. Any smoker knows how hard it is to quit, but I'd never had a cigarette on my lips, and the nicotine smell was unpleasant. She was immersed in arguments: against me because of my demand to stop smoking, against herself because she felt impotent and somewhat ashamed knowing I was right, and against the cigarette itself, which she squashed in the ashtray. It was hard to understand how a non-smoking male had fallen so much in love with a smoking female. Gladys was very special, though. For a non-smoker, it is very easy to critically and strongly judge and condemn a smoker. One should try to be in the smoker's shoes and ask the individual how and why he/she started the addiction and whether he/she had tried to stop smoking. At the end of the day, one is a human being and it is good to pour empathy into our judgments. Knowing the initial reason for smoking helps us understand how the addiction started and whether it is possible to do away with.

After she had smoked for more than forty years she complained to the doctor about frequent colds. The physician showed Gladys the last X-ray that indicated shadows in the lungs. He had uselessly recommended several times that she quit smoking. This last time, though, he demanded that she stop the addiction. The sickness had grown considerably worse.

That same day, she sat down alone in the living room staring at a box of cigarettes with which she started a monologue. She needed to be alone. She did not want to hide the box and pretend that she had overcome the addiction. During some days she had been doing so, and finally she stopped smoking. These events had taken place four years prior. It appears that this decision should have been done earlier. The damage had already been done and was irreversible.

My mind also went back to very happy times. I distinctly remembered our three-day stay in Budapest, Hungary. The tourist group was riding in a boat along the river dividing the city between the Buda and the Pest sections. The boat stopped in front of the Hungarian Parliamentary House, a true gothic jewel. Having this building as a backdrop on the pleasant summer night, we felt so happy and elated that I embraced and kissed her. I told her with my eyes, my whole body, how much I loved her! It was as if there was no one else besides us. It was blissful! We were radiantly happy!

There was another moment at the Madrid Royal Palace. It was a huge esplanade lit up by the sun under blue skies on a pleasant summer day. We were holding our hands, singing romantic songs, walking around. After a while we reached one end of the square and sat on a bench. Then a young man approached us with a camera in one hand asking for permission to take a photo of us. We were surprised at the request and asked him the reason. He told us that he had been inspired with the love we felt for each other, not very common in a middle-aged couple, and wanted to keep it as a souvenir.

An interesting example took place in Dubai. We were part of a group of tourists during five days in December 2014. At the end of the trip, one Latin American lady got closer to and congratulated us for being the only couple holding hands all the time. We were not interested in showing our innermost feelings to other people, but we always felt the need to hold hands, whether we were seated in a bus, on a train, on an airplane, or at home watching TV. There was a sort of magnet between our hands that resisted being separate.

All these thoughts were going through my mind. An idea occurred to me—I felt the need to share our special love relationship and to spread the word about Gladys' exceptionalism. I also needed to fight against my grief. It became compulsory for me to write about her, her internal beauty, her virtues and shortcomings as a human being. As an inborn professor, I was used to insatiably learning and spreading knowledge. I could not keep the knowledge inside of me and needed to make it known to other people.

For forty years I was blessed to share my life with an extraordinary person. Her life can be inspiring to many human beings in this same world full of wars, miseries, terrorist threats, hatred, and conflicts. There is also tenderness on this planet. We have to discover this wonderful feeling in ourselves, our families, and our friends and to enjoy it as long as there is life. It will comfort us in times of grief. To love and to be loved is a big human achievement. Gladys showed me what real love is, and I want to share this knowledge. I will delve deep into her virtues, all of them directly or indirectly related to this magnificent feeling of tenderness. Come on. Join me on this adventure.

# CHAPTER I -
# HER LOYALTY AND SINCERITY

I got married for the first time in my early twenties without any prior serious romantic relationships. I unfortunately chose a young woman whose intellectual horizons were vastly different from mine. As time went by, the disparities between us grew bigger, to the point of lacking common topics to talk about. We got married in 1962 and divorced in 1972. At that moment I became a bachelor, intensely enjoying life and looking for pleasure and company, but—after some crazy years—I knew I needed to learn what real love was. I wouldn't find out until February 1975.

It was a summer-like Cuban winter with high temperatures that did not justify wearing even the lightest coat. Men were wearing *guayaberas,* or long-sleeved shirts, only on solemn occasions. The day of my first serious rendez-vous was deliciously breezy, somewhat cloudy under a typically Cuban sky. The sun was caressing rather than heating the skin. The author of this book was seated at a table in Coppelia, the most famous Havana ice cream parlor. Its installations were located in a whole block at the heart at downtown Havana.

I was seated at a table on the patio, and the branches of a nearby tree provided me with some shade. I was waiting for a lady with whom I had made a date. In the process of getting comfortable in a cozy chair with semicircular back support, my attention was suddenly arrested by an elegantly beautiful lady, modestly dressed in a blue feminine suit with a skirt discreetly revealing a pair of beautiful legs. She was slowly getting closer to me. Isn't this scene familiar to the reader?

Wow! The encounter lasted for several hours, which went by so smoothly and quickly that I did not realize that the afternoon had turned to twilight, and later to night. I was not aware of the moment when the sun disappeared and the moon appeared in the starry Havana sky. I assume that there were people walking around us, but my attention was not fixed on them. Gladys was doing almost all the talking.

I was fascinated while unsuccessfully trying to reach her hands and arms. Her lips appeared to be like roses in front of my eyes. She was letting me know about her childhood and early adult life in the countryside with grandparents, aunts, and uncles, and—finally—the unfortunate marriage in which she had been unhappily living for five years. My manhood misconstrued the oral signal and relaunched an attack at the same time that she increased resistance. Her voice resembled that of an artist in a radio-broadcast soap opera. I was bewildered! One cannot easily understand how a woman having a rendezvous with a man starts talking about divorce while at the same rejecting his attempts to kiss her. What was the point of the confession? I was even more confused when she—then—told me that she had the hunch or impression that she would fall in love with me and that I might be the man in her life. That was it!

At that moment, Gladys inclined herself toward me, seriously staring at my eyes and told me that she could not betray or lie to anybody. My amazing new friend could not be unfaithful to either her husband or me. She could not offend him by being my girlfriend, even though if he touched her, she would feel uncomfortable, like she was being unfaithful to me. Gladys did not know how, but she had to get divorced as soon as possible. She could not kiss or go out with me before getting divorced. She slowly stood up with a smile on her face and said:

—As soon as I get divorced, I will contact you.

For several days, I had Gladys on my mind in a mixture of surprise, frustration, and admiration. Approximately three weeks after the rendezvous, she called me and we agreed to meet the following day.

After greeting me with a "Good evening," she immediately handed me the divorce certificate. It was issued the same day on which she'd phoned me. That night was one of the happiest of my life.

It was the encounter of the man and the woman, the gentleman's conquest of the lady who was spiritually virgin. Antonio was the first lover in her life, and she was discovering a new world, not only for her, but also for him. Both of them felt the combination of desire and love. The connection of the bodies was simultaneously happening with the linking of the souls. The body language was stronger than words. The true meaning of marriage was revealed to them. Words could not express the joy sparkling in their eyes. It was the intercourse of their souls! How could Antonio have imagined—then—that the beautiful woman he was holding in his arms would become his soul mate, the most important human being in his life for the next four decades?

Staring at me, Gladys told me that she did not accept betrayal. If she became my girlfriend, she would not tolerate any sort of competition. I assured her that I would be faithful—at that time, I had been going out with another woman, but there was no comparison with Gladys. I decided to break off my relationship with the previous lady and to dedicate myself totally to my new girlfriend. I was not courageous enough to tell my fair lady—then— about my previous love affair, and that, as matter of fact, I abruptly broke up with her the following day through a telephone call. The other woman was surprised but accepted my decision: I was doing this so as to not lose Gladys.

A deep respect for her integrity was added to the overwhelmingly physical attraction to her.

My curiosity about the origin of Gladys' rejection for falsehood or even hiding a truth was satisfied while we lived for two years in her grandparents' house. In that home, it was easy to feel an environment of principles and values clearly in opposition to lies. The aunts would talk to me about their niece's childhood. Since she was a little girl, she knew that mischief was not allowed by the family; if they misbehaved and were discovered, instead of confessing upfront, the punishment was more severe.

This gentleman was not like Gladys. Lies came from my mouth every now and then. Before getting married, I had a brief love affair with a stewardess in a flight from Havana to Camagüey, which was 500 kilometers away. I stayed five days in the previously-mentioned city. Immediately after my arrival, I called Gladys by phone. After the first minutes of the conversation she asked me the name of the woman with whom I had been unfaithful to her. I was astonished. How did she know? Who could have been the informant? I did not remember seeing anyone I knew on the flight. For several days Gladys asked me the same question, and I answered in the same way. Finally, I had to give up and confess my crime.

Gladys explained that from the very beginning of that first phone conversation, she'd realized that I had been unfaithful by the tone of my voice when I greeted her. She could tell that my speech did not express the same eagerness to have sex in the way she was used to perceiving it from me. The only explanation she could reason out was that I had had intercourse with a lady in Camagüey. She was bothering me constantly for some days, reminding me of my incorrect behavior. After some days, Gladys realized that I had seriously repented and then she decided to forgive me. The consequences of lying became crystal clear to me. If I had confessed my betrayal from the beginning, the punishment would have been less severe. I also noticed that I had unwillingly made her suffer, and not doing that was very important for me. She did not deserve my bad behavior. To imagine how much she had cried due to my error was the true punishment.

Years went by and Gladys' sincerity and love were reinforced by impeccable conduct, always honest and true. I could feel that there was a correspondence between words and actions. I never saw a contradiction or anything wrong that she had not told me about. She was very consistent in her behavior. The only surprises that I received were the unexpected discoveries of new virtues: for example the straightway of accepting mistakes that were incorrectly attributed to other people. She could not have peace of mind in knowing that somebody else had been accused of a mistake Gladys had made, even if that person was not a friend.

During the forty years we spent together in Cuba, Mexico, and the United States, I could ratify her honest position as long as work relations with bosses or coworkers were concerned. Sometimes she had to go through unpleasant situations, but never—as far as I knew—felt ashamed for having lied or hidden any wrong behavior. She preferred to get angry and face reprimands once and for all rather than hiding behind a lie that would indirectly protect her. Gladys never agreed with any shameless behavior, regardless of who was the guilty one. My lady's face would be red with anger whenever she felt cheated!

Her rejection of lies was so innate that she was able to foretell the false bits of human nature even if they were disguised. However, she never liked to scorn or hurt anybody whose lie had been uncovered. My fair lady could even be somewhat compassionate in trying to discover the reason for the falsehood and to offer some sort of empathy. She always preferred an unpleasant and poignant truth to a pious lie, especially related to health problems. Gladys knew how to combine bad news with kindness, compassion, and empathy. She was kind, careful, and tender in expressing negative messages.

I had a different approach and preferred not to tell her about pain, discomfort, or otherwise poor health, preferring instead to keep it secret up to the moment of consulting with a physician. I did not want to worry her before being certain of having a real problem.

I was also letting Gladys know the way I intended to start to solve the issue.

She did not approve of this behavior because, in her view, it was similar to hiding the problem, inciting a lack of confidence. She needed to trust in me completely, without any reservation, and wanted to be aware of even the slightest health problem I might be experiencing. Gladys' way of thinking strengthened and confirmed my absolute trust in her.

How can one be uncertain about a wife's love when she tenderly looks at you—eye to eye—with a smile on her face, holding your hands, and whispering how great was her love? During our forty years of togetherness, I never, ever, doubted her commitment to me. Gladys' open and honest attitude considerably improved my own sincerity. She was an open book for me and made it possible for me to become an open book for her. My lady's faithfulness grew the need in me to follow her example and become a better human being.

It is quite unusual for sincerity and loyalty to be delivered with tenderness and compassion. Gladys waited for the right moment to show disapproval of any inadequate behavior. She drew the person to be criticized to a private place, without any witness, and firmly but kindly expressed disapproval, including some possible negative consequences of the misconduct.

On several occasions, she had to call my attention to blunt gestures, violent reactions, or incorrect treatment in pointing out shortcomings to individuals making mistakes. Her clear explanation of conscious or unconscious wrong attitudes created in me the need for reasoning and interiorizing specific events. I learned to sincerely apologize for my mistakes, regardless of my honest intentions. It is not pleasant to ask for forgiveness. However, how rewarding is the satisfaction of being forgiven! Does this sound familiar to the reader?

Gladys was the poster child of honesty and sincerity intertwined with compassion and empathy. I learned a lot from her!

# CHAPTER II -
## GLADYS' INTERACTION
## WITH JEALOUSY

The man felt somewhat uneasy. His imagination was running wild because of unconfirmed but assumed tragic outcomes that went on and on in his mind. She regularly called him at this time, but the phone had yet to ring. Was she shopping or visiting her girl-friends—or was it a male friend? He did not clearly remember whether his lady had told him of any special outing. As a matter of fact, he had already been waiting for more than half an hour and no calls have been received. Had something happened to her? So far he had not learned about anybody else's presence in her life. Was she angry because of his rejecting her invitation to go shopping two days earlier?

All of a sudden—finally—the phone rang. Gracious Christ! He hurried up, grabbed the phone, did not identify the number, and heard a voice from the other side of the line. It was her! He started scolding her for the delay. There was no chance of making him listen. She tried to explain, but he constantly interrupted her. After some minutes, she was finally allowed to apologize for not having called at the agreed time because she'd forgotten both her cell and her watch at home. She'd asked somebody for help and was calling from the other person's phone.

Despite her excuses, he was still angry. She repeated the apology but to no avail. He – then - saw her watch and her cell phone on top of a chair. He realized he had been unfair to his lady. At the end of the day, he had gotten angry for the fun of it!

One can be jealous, untruthful, and uneasy without any real motive. What is the reason? Is there a real or imaginary issue? Why is it possible to lose control of oneself? During our long love relationship, we had experienced very few incidents of jealousy. Gladys never gave me a reason to be worried about her truthfulness—despite being a very beautiful woman—because she was always an open book for me. It never occurred to me that she would be able to betray.

I must admit that I did not have a flawless record, which she was aware of. She knew me so well that she would readily notice any irregular behavior: nobody had to inform her. She never had to search the pockets of my trousers looking for some clue of disloyalty. She faced disloyalty with anger, indignation, and pain but remained firm and sure of herself. I knew that she was right and did not have a reasonable argument or even an excuse at hand. She was aware of the fact that some men justify their treason on the basis of cultural misconceptions, such as 'playing the manly role,' *machista* excuses or weakness of our general attraction to women, especially if they are young and well-shaped. Her forgiveness to my trespass was conditional to the non-repetition of the action.

In my experience, love relationships can be characterized by different stages and degrees of togetherness. When I was thirty-five, some months after meeting Gladys, I was more attracted to sex than to love itself. This is the stage in which, from a male point of view, love has not been consolidated beyond the corporal appeal. A man can easily yield to the temptation of going on a new adventure as long as he believes—or wants to believe—that his wife does not know. He would not want to be bothered with her jealousy.

The ego was in the center of attention: my satisfaction, my pleasure, my feeling of being a real man able to please more than one woman.

When I turned forty and was doing scientific research in the former Soviet Union for a nine-month stay, during the first five months I had not gotten together with any female although my virility made me yearn to do so. At the sixth month, I happened to meet a middle-aged attractive lady for whom it was easy to get my attention. A temporary relief of my anxiety.

I thought my wife would never learn of my trespass which had taken place thousand miles across the Atlantic Ocean and going south to the Caribbean Sea. I knew my male colleagues wouldn't tell her. Men protect other men's secretive lives with women. It would be considered unmanly to denounce another man's adventures.

When after my nine-month absence I returned to Cuba my wife was waiting for me, her arms wide opened ready to hug me. During our first intercourse, I felt a strange feeling of change. I had gotten used to being in bed with a larger feminine anatomy.

Gladys' intuition and sagacity meant she understood what was going on with me, and, in a low tone and measuredly broken voice, told me that it was hard for her to understand how she had been able to live without a man—for nine months—when she was thirty some years old. She said she was comforted simply by smelling her man's odor in the sheet and pillow cover which she had not washed for nine months. She slept hugging and kissing the pillow on my bedside to feel close to me.

I was ashamed of my behavior because I was making her suffer in front of my very eyes. I could not forgive myself. From that moment on, I had to think more about her than about myself. I felt that my love for her did not match her love for me. From the bottom of my heart, shedding tears of repentance, I asked her, please, to forgive me. She hugged me and started to cry.

It was a very hard blow for Gladys to have seen and verified my disloyalty. She did not quickly recover from the impact on her most intimate feelings. Normally her reaction to violent outcomes was slower than mine. On September 11, 2001, she was shocked for more than a month. It was terrible to witness young people committing suicide by throwing themselves through the windows of the Twin Towers in Manhattan to avoid being carbonized. She was trembling and crying for a long time. She needed a psychologist's help to get over the tragedy. I was also impacted by the violent terrorist attacks, especially the scenes of the planes flying into the buildings and making them tumble down, but I recovered in a matter of days and resumed teaching.

She was considerably confused and sad. She did not argue with me, did not ask for any explanation, was not jealous of me, and did not talk to me in a resentful way. She was silently suffering and sad. I was facing an internal dilemma. I felt deeply guilty and did not know how to mitigate my stern self-accusation. I was in the middle of an impasse, unconsciously and irresponsibly created by me. I tried to appease her but did not know how. Flowers could not be a way to make her happy. I was afraid of making things worse.

I felt sure that she was observing my strange behavior. She herself took care of solving the conflict. One morning she woke me up with kisses and told me,

—Our love has survived this crossroad. Nothing happened when you were in Kiev.

I couldn't help sobbing and holding her in my arms, unstoppably kissing my dearest wife.

As a matter of fact, men and women have different—and sometimes opposite—standpoints about relationship "love-jealousy." Cultural and idiosyncratic differences among nations, throughout centuries, also play important roles as far as the interaction between these two emotions is concerned.

On Wikipedia, one can read the following definition: "Jealousy is an emotion, and the word typically refers to the thoughts and feelings

10

of insecurity, fear, concern, and anxiety over an anticipated loss of status or something of great personal value, particularly in reference to a human connection."

On the basis of my interaction with women since I was eighteen years old, I agree with the above definition, which excludes the word 'love.' This gentleman thinks that when love between partners reaches the stage of soul mates, when each of them thinks first about the other before him or herself. Especially when the feeling of love goes beyond the body (or when sexual relations rarely exist because of old age or lack of health), *at this point in time* there is no room for jealousy.

When the main focus of a couple is the satisfaction of physical desire, it is possible—especially for a man—to get tired of that specific person and to try another one that might have a better shape, prettier face, or a slenderer body. At that stage, the souls might have not been completely integrated. It is possible to find similarities between bodies, but it is much harder to find them between souls. When a fully realized love exists in a couple, there must be a two-fold confidence and respect: in your lover and in yourself. To falsely accuse one of infidelity is an insult to any member of a fully loving couple.

When the love relationship in a couple is in the initial stage of passion, the physical attraction is the preponderant force keeping the couple together. The beauty of the body is extremely important, especially during youth when the hair almost totally keeps its natural color, the flesh is strong, and the skin is smooth and free of wrinkles. In this stage sex is very frequent, clothing becomes sometimes bothersome, and sex is urgent. Hormones and adrenaline are fully activated, and there is often not enough time to satisfy our desires completely.

This stage of love is quite common in a young couple who have recently initiated a romantic love affair; however, if this stage is not succeeded by another one identifying commonality of feelings, points of view, and spiritual standpoints, if there is no communion

11

between body and soul, if the ego is overwhelmingly imposed on the relationship by one member of the couple, if the preferences of going together and enjoying life are strikingly different, one or both may look for another partner. The members of a couple should have differences that would be welcome as long as they are complementary.

This author's opinion is that the passionate stage may be brittle because it might lack spiritual and intellectual interconnections, compatibilities in crucial components such as values, moral principles, similarity of socio-politico-economic and cultural preferences, and, of course, priorities in life. If the connection is only physical, the most beautiful and perfect bodies and faces may get boring. There may be the need to find other persons similarly attractive or even less attractive, but they will be new, ready to be discovered.

It is hard to prove the cause-effect relationship between love and jealousy. One can be deeply in love and not be jealous, as was the case of my wife's and many other people I have met in different countries. I had also met very jealous people who led very unstable sexual lives, constantly changing partners. Sometimes I have come to the conclusion—coinciding with the Wikipedia entry—that one of the causes of jealousy is insecurity.

I can add to this subject of conversation that in my personal case, going back in time, I remember the precise moment in which I knew that my love for Gladys had transcended the passionate stage: the day she gave me the option of either formalizing our relationship or putting an end to it. I could not leave her. This was the first time that I experienced that glorious feeling. Something deep inside told me that it would be impossible to live without her.

Jealousy doesn't lead to happiness in the couple, nor to stability or continuity in the love relationship. Gladys Morales proved that, through actions and words, one can be deeply in love with another person and never feel jealousy. There are couples who spoil lovely moments with arguments related to jealousy, even on unjustified occasions. To be jealous doesn't show love but rather resentment, lack of confidence, and insecurity.

In the context of differences between men and women, it is interesting to compare the respect in relationships by witnessing one's partner being sexually harassed by another person. Let us analyze the case when another individual shows attraction to your partner.

If the reader is a man, and all of a sudden he visualizes a fascinating lady who is accompanied by another man—regardless of the existing relationship between them—most likely he would not dare to stare at her in a luscious way or compliment her beauty aloud, knowing that he risks being beaten by the other man. We respect other men because we might lash out violently when our manhood is hurt. The harassment of our partner or companion in front of us is an insult to which no man can be indifferent.

As far as ladies are concerned, however, I have observed a different reaction. I have witnessed in my youth that once, accompanied by my wife, a woman had been looking at me in a provocative way, silently inviting me to approach her. My intelligent wife readily became aware of the situation, and her reaction was to expressively hug and kiss me. The other lady all of a sudden stopped staring at me. Education and principles wouldn't allow my wife to respond and insult the offender.

According to Gladys, there are at least two conditions which are necessary for loving one person intimately: number one, to respect and admire him, and number two, to love him. Does the reader agree with my wife that it is not possible to love a person whom you won't respect? You may respect a person and admire her, but will not necessarily fall in love with her. But if you love somebody, you cannot consciously make her suffer with your behavior. One must believe in that person and have confidence and respect. Jealousy should never be a topic to argue about in a true love relationship.

Gladys was very beautiful externally but also extremely precious and radiant inwardly. Her feelings were incomparably better than mine and constituted the strongest reason to stay by her until death separated us. Nonetheless, now nine months after her loss, I can assert that death did not separate us because she is deep inside of me. Her remains are at home in an urn on top of the dining table, and every day I kiss and embrace the little box. When my time comes to leave this world, our two urns will be placed one beside the other in a niche in our church. Forever!

# CHAPTER III -
# HER STRUGGLE TO
# IMPROVE HER MAN

It was a summer afternoon in the city of Havana, Cuba, in 1944. A lady in her thirties was taking a look at the shoe display in the window of a department store at the corner of Aguila and Monte streets while holding a child's hand. There were many people walking around them while buses and cars were going to and fro. Some cars were not respecting the traffic lights. Pedestrians had to be cautious because the transit of buses, cars, and bicycles was intense at the crossroad. The boy was actively moving in an effort to get free from his mother. Some moments later a young lady joined the group paying attention to the exhibition of shoes, saw the infant and addressed him. He was smiling while the young lady was talking to the mother and the child.

All of a sudden, the boy escaped from his mother's hand, raised the lady's skirt, spanked her buttocks, and started to soundly laugh. The mother—absolutely embarrassed by the child' behavior—immediately grabbed him and strongly scolded him while apologizing to the lady, who in seconds reacted from being surprised to insulted. She did not appear to accept the mother's excuses and accused the child of being spoiled and badly educated. Under those shameful circumstances, Siria Pita violently grabbed Antonio by his waist, went away from the store, saw a taxi standing in front of the red traffic light, and got into it.

Some minutes later, the taxi stopped in front of a masonry house. Siria and Antonio entered the house and met a middle-aged man in the living room. The mother was complaining to the father about the child's behavior at the store. Her face was red and considerably embarrassed. However, Florentino did not appear to be concerned; he started laughing and praising the boy's attitude. Siria was flabbergasted. There was no punishment for the child, who immediately started to run inside the house. Antonio was the youngest child of the four siblings and was lucky enough to be born at a turning point in the Morales-Pita's family economy. Florentino had won the lottery on two occasions shortly after Antonio was born. He was the only child to be raised by a nanny, who helped him to enjoy a childhood that satisfied all his whims. The Morales-Pitas had raised a deeply spoiled child.

Siria was born in a very poor family unable to send their daughters to school. She was a housewife and was never allowed to work outside home—she could only work in a local artisan sewing shop creating toddlers' clothes after her husband's demise when she turned sixty-eight years old; however, she had an inborn love for studying and for learning about nature and her surrounding world. She took care of educating her four children. She visited their school every week. While she could never have helped the children with their homework, she was an example in educational activities.

Besides being a spoiled child, Antonio also was very loving. He kissed his mother constantly. He loved to give her flowers and perfumes (bought by his father, of course) and showed his love for her with words and actions. On purpose, he did not hurt anyone and managed to be his mother's pet. He became her favorite child, not only for being kind, but also because he loved studying. Siria never had to remind Antonio about his homework. He exceeded all her educational expectations from a very young age. He was always asking his godfather for books. He loved reading, learning, and studying. Readers of my book *Havana-Merida-Chicago (A Journey to Freedom)* may remember his struggles for learning English and getting his baccalaureate, master's, and doctoral degrees.

The child soon became a young man. He started to work when he turned sixteen, was the first offspring to travel abroad based on his own savings, and learned how to speak Italian because his first boss was an Italo-American manager of El Mundo newspaper.

Antonio was handsome and kind to women, especially those who were much older than he. So he had several mature girlfriends who contributed to make him both a self-confident egoist, and a kind gentleman.

Siria was concerned with her son's attraction to women and was afraid of his committing himself not with a virgin, but with a divorced woman, such as he was dating. She equated female virginity with a decent marriage. He unexpectedly met a lady of the type recommended by his mother at his workplace. She was beautiful, only four years older than he, and she shared his political points of view at the time. Without really knowing what he was doing and pressed by his mother—who offered him the best room in the house to live with his future wife—Antonio got married within six months. During the ten years of that first marriage, he dedicated himself to his work and never took care of any chore at home, never even doing dishes. He was raised in the belief that he was more or less a conceited superman who simultaneously was happy, reasonably kind, naïve, and loving.

Let me now turn to Gladys.

Sitting on a bus from Havana from Menocal, where she was living since her divorce in February 1975, Gladys was looking out at the countryside and villages while a breeze caressed her face. She felt nervous and anxious but happy because she was going to meet Antonio, who almost every day accompanied her from the bus's first stop in Havana to her office. She had recently experienced a deep change from sharing her life with an unwanted husband she did not love to initiate a charming love affair with Antonio.

She felt strongly attracted to Antonio, whom she still did not deeply know. She had realized that he was somewhat of an egoist, but at the same time, he was loving, kind, and attentive to detail. They had so far been together for some months; however, there had not been any conversation about making the relationship official, meeting each other's families, or getting married. She did not know how to start a conversation about marriage with him. Neither of them had a ring; nonetheless, she was so extremely happy in his arms. He had developed in her the feeling of being a woman.

The bus made its final stop. The lady was descending from the vehicle at the very moment when she saw a familiar hand extended to her. Antonio was there with the usual smile on his face, welcoming her to Havana. They could not resist the temptation of a hug.

From the very beginning of the relationship, Antonio was aware of the fact that Gladys had some uncommon virtues, such as trying to improve him in a social context and to advise him on the best ways to get along with people. In a very intelligent way, she was struggling against his ego in the happiest moments, when he was in heaven. When Antonio was still immersed in love ecstasies, she started her criticism and advice about improving his relationships with other people. Arguments appeared in these interchanges of ideas. He was upset by the conversation, but at the end of the day, her sweetness came back and mesmerized him. She scolded Antonio with unpleasant remarks which were intertwined with one hug, two hugs, one kiss, a second kiss, tenderness, and love. So the argument would temporarily disappear until another day; when the argument resumed, he was caught off guard.

None of the previous women he had ever dated made him feel uncomfortable with criticism, but amidst the stress, he could feel a strange sensation of gratefulness. At first he was not aware that criticism was a way to make a better man out of him. Later on, he started to meditate that this attack actually was a manifestation of love. Yes, Gladys' love was very special, unique in many ways.

It is hard for a man to analyze and to accept a criticism at the time that he was feeling in paradise. However, it is also difficult for a woman in love, one — who had been raised in a very healthy and considerate home environment — to go against her principles of improving the man in her life, recognizing also that he had big virtues and that she felt a deep respect for him. She preferred to help Antonio and get somewhat upset rather than being apparently happy with an internal remorse for her inhibition.

Antonio's dilemma was to either go against his ego, which was stubbornly resisting pressure from Gladys, and consequently getting angry and uncomfortable, or to be understanding and grateful to the person who expressed part of her love for him by hammering his pride. At the end of the day, this was a crash between two people raised up in absolutely different home environments. Little by little, Antonio started to understand. He felt absolutely sure of his wife's love. There was no question about it.

Some months later, the time had come to make a decision about the love affair. Antonio felt comfortable being a boyfriend, but Gladys needed to make things official. This was not easy for her, but she offered him two options: 1) to initiate the process of formalizing their love status or 2) to put an end to the love affair. They had just been together for a couple of hours in a nearby hostel. She gave him one week to make the choice. This conversation took place on an autumn day on a beautiful afternoon under blue skies in a Havana park. She would, then, return to her Menocal home, and Antonio would go to his in Havana. There were no intertwined hands. She went away in search for a bus while Antonio was seated on a bench, deeply mediating on the dilemma.

Antonio was holding his head in his hands. He was so happy with Gladys, to whom he was totally dedicated. He had already met the woman in his life, but the idea of getting married was not there yet.

There were several question marks in relation to the compatibility between the two families, the choice of residence, the economic need for the financing of the marriage, the adjustment between two different personalities—to meet every now and then is not the same as sharing lives together. Complicating matters further, in Communist Cuba, it was almost impossible to find a second job. Would they be a happy married couple? For how long? He was against short marriages.

Nonetheless, one thing was crystal clear to Antonio. He was in love with Gladys and did not want to lose her. This would not be the first time that he had to put an end to a love affair. He was usually the one who took the initiative, but he had never felt so identified with a partner, and it was not hard for him to let girlfriends go. Now the situation was different. He could not let Gladys go. For the first time in his life, he felt unable to let a girl go! It actually did not matter that she interrupted the loveliest moments with criticisms about his personality. He loved and respected her because of her uniqueness. She was a true lady immersed in unusual honesty. — She was so beautiful.

Gladys walked slower after their farewell without caresses. She was afraid to lose him. Then she was walking slowly. She wanted to go back and kiss him, but she needed him to make a decision. She could not bear the idea of being only his girlfriend. The informal situation was deemed to be over sooner or later. It was almost a year since their unforgettable rendezvous at Coppelia. What a lovely year she had experienced being Antonio's girlfriend! She boarded the first bus that would take her to the Cordoba Park where, after standing in line for twenty or thirty minutes, she would board the bus to Menocal.

Antonio continued being immersed in his thoughts. All of a sudden he stood up. He had decided not to wait for a week. He was ready to share his life with her. He simply did not want to live without her. He would have taken a taxi, but that wasn't an option at the time in

Havana, whose transportation system was quite deficient. He had to get to the Cordoba Park before Gladys had boarded the 38 bus. He was lucky, though, because he did not need to wait too long for the 74 bus going from the Ciudad Deportiva to Acosta Street, from which he could walk to the Park. Once the 74 bus arrived at Acosta Street, he went running to the Cordoba Park and could see her in the process of boarding the bus. Without any introduction, he embraced and kissed her. Love had miraculously transformed a week into a couple of hours.

Approximately a year after their first rendezvous, Gladys and Antonio were married in a very modest ceremony, witnessed by the two families, a few close friends, and Antonio's children from his first marriage. Not all faces were happy. Siria Pita was somewhat racist, and Gladys was not white. Antonio's children's faces reflected uncertainty. This was not the first time that they had met their father's fiancée, but now the encounter was more official. They also met a large part of her family for the first time that day. Now it was for certain that their father would be sleeping with another woman and would never go back home as he used to three years earlier.

After a week-long honeymoon in a tourist resort in Ciénaga de Zapata, less than 100 kilometers from Havana, the newly married couple moved to one small maid bedroom with bath and kitchen in Antonio's elder sister's home in downtown Havana. This was their only possibility of living together. Their stay there lasted approximately two years.

Marriage did not completely reduce Gladys' sermons—or rather, homilies. Time went by and she was still insisting on introducing changes in my personality. At times, she was quite demanding and went back to the same issues that had not yet been totally solved, even though I had admitted that she was right. She called my attention to some mistakes in the family's social graces, such as the way of eating, especially the noises I made while eating soup. I found these requests somewhat unnecessary at home.

One evening, while waiting for her return home, I sat down, talking to myself, making some deductions. Recently Gladys had told me about my big virtues and missteps. She had even mentioned that some of my students commented that I was a great teacher but too exacting. I was good inwardly but not outwardly. It appeared as if it were hard for me to show compassion or empathy. As a conclusion, looking at my eyes with understanding, one day Gladys told me,

—Antonio, you are like a tarnished diamond.

There was something special about her recriminations. Never had she made a negative comment in front of other people, even a family member. Interestingly enough, if anybody criticized me in front of her, she immediately asked the individual whether he/she had ever talked to me directly about the issue. If the answer was no, then she insisted in bringing the comment directly to me so that I could know and maybe rectify the supposedly mistaken procedure. She was like a soldier defending her lieutenant. She was not a messenger, but his wife.

I wondered: why does she do it? Her intent was not to bother me, but I was certainly not happy listening to the remarks. She showed her love to me with her eyes, words, and actions, by sharing good and bad experiences, in asking for my help, and taking care of me whenever I felt slightly sick. She was able to manage working the whole day in an office, studying at the university in the evenings, and cooking delicious dinners—at the time my hunger was not easily satiated. I started to do some household chores which I had never done, such as doing the dishes, sweeping the floor, and scrubbing the bathroom, which always had to be impeccably clean. The interesting thing about this change is that it came voluntarily from me because I saw how busy my wife was. Gladys had created in me the need to share the load, and to be tender with her.

I went through more changes at that time as well. I was totally dependable, in charge of getting the rationed food at our assigned supermarket. Before meeting her, I did not pay attention to what other individuals thought about me or if any of my actions would bother anybody else. I started to feel as if I were a somewhat different man—a better one.

I had always strictly fulfilled my duties, especially as a professor and a scholar. At the same time, I was very demanding with other people regardless of whether or not they were accountable to me. My wife always recommended me to introduce understanding into my requests, to try to be in the other persons' shoes, and not to hurt their feelings. I was improving my conduct. Gladys admired my perseverance and ability to overcome obstacles; therefore, she then asked me to include compassion in my passion to work and to fight.

As time went by, the changes were extended to interpersonal relations as the couple made decisions together, without imposing points of view on the other partner, sharing and discussing opinions and points of view.

In 2002, after saving money for some years in Chicago, we were able to visit Italy as tourists. I took care of coordinating all actions: choosing the cities, the hotels, the flights, and the excursions. She had been unconsciously denied of having an opinion, and she protested. It was true, she said, that I had assumed all expenditures, but that did not give me the right to place her in a position of accepting whatever was my decision. It was agreed between the two of us that from that moment, whenever we were going to fly, everything had to be coordinated between the two of us. Little by little, I was adapting myself to share responsibilities. My higher level of income did not give the right to impose my will. The "*machista*" Antonio was slowly turning into a family man, and, consequently, being more respected academically and socially. Now his students got closer to him as well.

On several occasions, we were involved in small arguments about banal issues and differences that were due to not understanding the behavior of the opposite sex. My wife was telling me that whenever we planned on going to any theater or social activity, she needed more time than I in order to get ready, and consequently, it was not fair for me to demand her to be faster; in reality, she was telling me that I was asking her to behave like a man, and she—of course—was not.

Slowly but firmly we were coming to understand that women and men have different mental structures. It is not whether a man is more or less intelligent, or physically or mentally stronger than a woman. It was not a matter of knowing who won an argument. The winner should be neither of them but the couple instead. When does this happen? This agreement takes place when both of them partially concedes to what each of them was strongly supporting, establishing a trade-off, in which both partially lose and win. This process takes place when they start assimilating the mutual advantages and disadvantages, seeing how their differences complement each other. At the end of the day, they end with a compromise, sealing it with a kiss and a loving smile. Both won! Love was the winner!

We were constantly interchanging points of view. She had a large analytical capacity and was able to talk about a variety of topics. She also had a very interesting way of getting her points across. We were recognizing the differences between our sexes and arrived at the conclusion that it was very hard, almost impossible, for a woman to understand a man's way of thinking, and for a man, it was equally difficult to comprehend a woman's reasoning structure. For example, as most women do, Gladys loved to receive flowers, especially when she was surprised because there was no special occasion in sight. I could never understand that feminine joy of receiving flowers. I recognized the beauty of flowers, but that was it. I just knew that my wife would be delighted to see me with a bunch of flowers in my hands when I opened the door.

All I wanted was to make her happy, not understanding the effect of flowers on her feelings. I just loved to see the glitter in her eyes, her beautiful smile, and the warm welcome with an endless hug. I remembered the days I defended my dissertations, when according to the Ukrainian custom, several bunches of tulips were handed to me. Although I was smiling and thankful, in reality I felt very uncomfortable because I did not know how to hold the flowers or whether I should smell their perfume. I wasn't happy at all and got rid of the flowers as soon as I was alone outside the building.

I invite the male reader to remember this advice: it doesn't matter if we can't understand feminine reasoning; the important fact is to know what makes them happy. Then, most likely, we pave the way for women to understand what makes us elated in turn.

My lovely soul mate was a very intelligent woman, able to delve deeply inside of me. Her self-assigned task of polishing my deficiencies was so successful that I was—as time went by—transforming myself into a better man. One really feels very well when there is peace and harmony at home. It was so nice to consult and to make decisions together although this coordination might entail a delay. We were voluntarily sharing responsibility and feeling that every decision was mutual. It was wonderful to make our home the reign of love, to which we are willing to arrive and to receive the love of our soul mate.

Another one of Gladys' influences on my personality was to teach me to accept reality, to face life as it was, regardless of how unfavorable it might be. By my own nature I am a fighter, an entrepreneur, who dislikes losing battles. Sometimes, regardless of how hard one might try to change a situation or how justified or logical the purpose might be, reality cannot be transformed. Readers of *Havana-Merida-Chicago (A Journey to Freedom)* may remember that after twenty-five years of doing my best to improve the Cuban sugar industry, I had to give up my dream. As can be seen in that book, thanks to Gladys' perseverance and patience, at the same time that doing what I could, I learned to accept that some ideals cannot be achieved. It's better to enjoy those objectives that were in fact doable.

Without exhausting all the benefits given to me by Gladys, I cannot forget her help in organizing my personal life by always knowing where I had left my keys, my cell phone, my wallet, or even my money. She insisted on several occasions that, before going out, I had to check my pockets to make sure that everything was in place and, of course, check the variable Chicago weather forecast. At the beginning, it took time to get used to keeping things in their place. The resulting benefits in stress and time are worthwhile. After several reminders—and some small arguments—I could put an end to avoidable stressful situations at the time of leaving home.

# CHAPTER IV -
# HER FIRMNESS, BRAVERY, PRINCIPLES, AND VALUES

After 1959, when Fidel Castro's revolution succeeded in Cuba, housing was—is and most likely will be—one of the most acute problems for the Cuban people. He established the politically correct but economically erroneous policy of slashing 50% of all rents. This measure undoubtedly was wholeheartedly approved by all, but it led to a contraction in the housing building industry—which was still in hands of the private sector—and at the same time, it created a huge increase in the demand for rental houses. The permanent establishment of fixed- and low-price renting, known as a "price ceiling" in economics, led to a deep shortage of housing that consistently worsened alongside the population increase.

My father was one of the landlords affected by this measure. When he won the lottery on two occasions, he could buy three houses and build a big one for his family. The Revolution took over the properties with a small compensation to the original homeowners that they were forced to accept, with the exception of the home that they used as a primary residence, which remained part of their property. Some years before 1959, my two sisters and my eldest brother got married and rented their own houses; therefore, I was living with my parents in the paternal home composed of four bedrooms, two bathrooms, one dining room, one kitchen, one living room, an entrance hall, and a backyard.

The reader may remember that I got married and my parents agreed to have my wife to live with us. Our family grew to four persons in the first four years of marriage. In the seventh year, though, shortly before traveling to Scotland to study, it became obvious to me that our marriage was definitely broken. My then wife came from Holguin, one of the eastern most provinces in Cuba, and—had we gotten divorced—she would have been forced to take the children with her away from Havana. I thus preferred to wait for the possibility of renting a home, giving it to my children, and returning to my parents' home. Luckily enough, when I got my master's degree in Glasgow, the Dean of the Department of Economics, as a recognition for becoming the first faculty (at the College of Economics), to get that graduate degree abroad, granted me the privilege of renting an apartment in the residential part of Havana.

A few months after starting renting the apartment, I could finally get divorced, give the house to my children and their mother, and return to my paternal home. There was, though, an unforeseen inconvenience for me. My parents had the idea of exchanging their big home for my brother's small home, which was composed of only two bedrooms. Each one of my parents slept in separate rooms; consequently, I had to sleep on a couch in the living room. Being single was not a problem for the following three years, until I met the love of my life.

For the first two years of living with my sister, everything was all right, but, at the beginning of the third year, I had a big argument with my sister, and Gladys and I had to pick up our belongings and leave the apartment in a couple of hours. In the early evening hours of that day, we were sitting in the garage on our scarce furniture figuring out where to go next.

Gladys and I were staring at one another. I was nervously scratching my head while she was apparently calm. She gave me the first lesson in bravery. There were neither complaints nor reproaches. My fair lady was stable and at peace while we were analyzing our choices. My mother's home was not an option. Siria Pita did not like Gladys, and there was the eternal contradiction between mother and daughter-in-law. Suddenly her beautiful eyes glittered, expressing joy and hope. She suggested moving to her aunts' home in Menocal.

I wasn't that optimistic because I was thinking about going through a round trip, Menocal-Havana, every week day and also on Saturdays, which I then dedicated to study with my children, and maybe twice per month to go places on Sundays. The transportation service was awful and meant commuting at least four hours per day. I had to wake up around five a.m. and return home after ten p.m. I wondered how many hours per day I would be able to sleep and—very importantly—at what time we could make love?

On top of that, what would it be like to live with her three aunts? Was there any other option? I couldn't work it out.

Gladys had an advantage over me. She was used to this daily round trip, would be returning to the home where she spent her childhood and early youth, and—much more than this—she deeply loved and knew her aunts. So far, I had been always willing to face challenges, but this time there was a big question mark in my brain. I would not be in my comfort zone, the only man living with a wife and three elderly women. This would definitely be a new stage in my life. Gladys' firmness helped me come to grips with the situation.

After a few moments, we came to the conclusion that living in Menocal was our only option. Gladys called her uncle Ramon, who lived in a Havana neighborhood, to help in transporting our belongings, and around 9 p.m., we arrived in Menocal. Because there was no phone available in Menocal, the aunts had not been alerted of our arrival; nonetheless, they opened their house to us.

The Núñez-Malvarez family's home was an example of mutual respect and peace among its members. The house was big, partly built with wood and masonry walls. A perfume of cleanliness, mixed with that of the flowers from the garden at the front of the house, pervaded the environment.

After struggling to fall asleep in the new bed, I finally opened my eyes. Gladys had woken up earlier and was looking at me with a smile on her face. We stared at each other, wondering how this new face of our marriage would be. She advised me that my underwear was to be worn only in our bedroom.

My brain was flooded with questions. She recognized my state of mind and asked me to be patient. Her workload would be increased because, in our new home, men were not allowed to cook, do the dishes, or sweep the floor. One of the aunts was in charge of going to the market to buy food. Gladys had nothing to do with the arguments with my sister; nonetheless, she was ready to take on the new tasks in order to keep our marriage together.

Teresa Núñez, despite being seated in a wheelchair, was in charge of handling the family's financial issues. She was the first aunt I met that first morning, and she welcomed me with a smile on her face and an extended friendly hand. We had been talking in the previous months after formalizing our marriage. Now I was facing the leader of the family. She was intelligent, talkative, and acutely aware of the Cuban economic situation. There was no mention of the reason for our impromptu move to their home. She was bravely fighting against an incurable sickness and keeping the family together after her parents died almost simultaneously after the Cuban revolutionary government had taken over a considerable piece of their property. We were talking about my job at the University of Havana and also about Gladys.

The three aunts were fond of the gentleman their niece had chosen as a husband. Gladys did not have to tell me how to behave. For the first time in my life, I was living in a truly respectful family environment. No monetary compensation was ever mentioned. It was taken for granted that I would—of course—do my best to help in any possible way. This was Gladys' cradle, where her character had been forged.

At the end of the day, we had a small and cozy place in which to live until it was possible to buy or rent a house of our own.

For a couple of years, every now and then we rented a room for the weekends or holidays in a hotel at Santa Cruz del Norte, a seaside town 30 kilometers east of Havana. She never complained about our difficulties and inspired me to do the same. Her bravery was contagious!

We were finally able to resolve our housing problem thanks to the physical and emotional sacrifices Gladys was subject to for three years. Every other Sunday she was, without receiving any monetary payment, building houses under the auspices of her employer, the Ministry of Building. My lady had finished her bachelor's degree and was working eight hours per day from Monday to Saturday morning as financial advisor at the aforementioned Ministry.

Knowing her deeply feminine nature as I did, it was hard to imagine her wearing gloves, holding bricks, placing layers of cement, or pulling a cart. This was a concrete example of her courage, principles, and values. She felt that our togetherness might have been affected if we could not solve our housing problem. When we had been married for five years, she was given an apartment with a low rent on the fifth floor of a building without an elevator in the western outskirts of Havana. At long last, we could be together in our own home!

Her bravery and courage also took center stage during our first year living in the United States because at that time she did not speak English. Gladys was studying very hard, day and night, and some mornings I would find that she had slept at the table. Her brain was educated to express words in complex sentences, not in simple ones. She felt that she needed to learn English in a similarly fluid and educated way.

The managers of La Posada, the Casa Central shelter where we were living upon arrival to the US while our immigration situation was being legalized, were astonished and inspired by Gladys' learning commitment. She was their poster child of the Hispanic community when it came to learning English. Immediately after receiving her social security number and the first work permit, she started to teach Spanish at the Berlitz Learning Center and also became a freelancer as a private instructor in our native language.

When we completed our first year, Gladys started to work as a GED instructor teaching mathematics at a private two-year college. Two years later, she had created her own methodology for teaching GED courses. When talking to the human resources director about helping her to publish the methodology, he offered her a raise in salary if she gave the copyright of the book to the college. Gladys was insulted by the option and left the college as soon as the course was over. Two months later, she got another job as a GED and Introduction to Business instructor in Spanish while still taking intensive English courses. After completing her fourth year in Chicago, the woman in my life became faculty of Introduction to Business in Spanish and English.

My wife was also firm and simultaneously sweet with my children, whose mother felt animosity for Gladys and transmitted that negative feeling to them. On one occasion, during the first months of our marriage, I rented an apartment with two bedrooms at Varadero beach. Although we were enjoying our honeymoon, Gladys agreed to share the apartment with my children because she knew how much I loved them.

Unexpectedly—and of course without any invitation—their mother visited a nearby apartment and made her presence known to us. She was wearing a white lacy swimsuit I had given her five years ago when I returned to Havana from Glasgow. Our happiness at the beach was short lived.

The children were hyperactive and inappropriately spoke to Gladys. They tried to bother her but she controlled her temper without agreeing with their mischievous behaviors. I called my children's attention to several occasions where my fair lady demanded respect and good manners. My daughter all of a sudden got sick and started to reject our attention. I had to take her to the nearby clinic. The situation was tense until their mother returned to Havana with them. After that storm, we could resume our happiness.

My wife was never invited to visit my children's home, and she would not have wanted to be where she was not welcomed. However, we invited my children to our home, where they behaved and kept their composure. They had to respect our home, where their mischievous behavior would not be tolerated. Gladys was able to be kind and forgiving as long as she was respected as my wife.

As far as political issues were concerned, the Cuban dictatorship's repression at all levels of society—openly exerted by the police and armed forces and somewhat disguised at the neighborhood, schools, and workplaces— did not allow any disagreement with the government. Cubans were criticized if they attended church, and Christmas celebrations were not allowed during several decades until Pope John II visited the island in the late 1990s. Gladys believed in God but preferred not to talk about it in public. Her principles and values did not allow her to accept impositions, even though they emanated from the Cuban Communist Party, which enjoyed privileges in our society.

In the early nineties, Gladys started to work in a governmental foreign trade enterprise as a specialist in financial-economic analysis. She was assigned the evaluation of substituting a domestic product by an imported one. Her analysis showed that to domestically elaborate the imported product was not economically justifiable because the amount of saved foreign currency by not importing the product was surpassed by the total dollar expenditure of imported components and raw materials required in its domestic output.

When she showed the results to her boss, he was disappointed and said that the domestic production had already been approved by his director. Gladys insisted on the economic inconvenience of the solution, while the boss replied that her results could not be verified.

Gladys' face was transformed with indignation. Her eyes expressed contempt for her boss' servile attitude in kneeling to his manager and accepting a decision that would damage the Cuban economy, which he was supposed to defend.

Gladys reiterated that she had finished a university career in finances and accounting, which had knowledge that enabled her to accomplish the research. She explicitly stated her position. Since my lady was professionally defending the Cuban economy, she was against the imposed decision. The boss stared at her in a sign of reproof, and with a simulated smile on his face, pointed to the office door.

From that moment on, the relations between them became tense. Some weeks later, he gladly agreed to let her go for a year to Mexico to do joint research with me. She was told that the position in the enterprise would be open to new candidates. It wasn't certain whether she would be rehired on her return to Cuba.

During the seven months I was detained in Cuba in 1995, I experienced a feeling similar to that of a man held in jail. The Cuban Ministry of Higher Education, in spite of having approved the extension of my contract with the Mexican government for the 1995-1996 academic year, did not renew my passport when in July 1995 I went to Cuba for one week to see my mother, who had become seriously ill.

I couldn't go back to Mexico and was forced to interrupt my research activity and to deprive two dozen Mexican undergraduate and graduate students of their teacher and mentor. As I explained in detail in *Havana-Merida-Chicago (A Journey to Freedom)*, Gladys' role was fundamental in getting me back to Mexico. My soul mate was, on a weekly basis, keeping me abreast of the events taking place in Mexico and insisting with my bosses in Yucatan to send faxes to the College of Economics of the University of Havana and demanding my return to Mexico, and later to the Mexican Embassy in Havana, so that the contracts could be fulfilled. Gladys was always firm and certain of my somewhat miraculous escape from Cuba. Had she not being in Mexico, my return would most likely have never happened.

Another surprise was waiting for us in February 1996, on my return to Merida. I readily contacted my former boss to see how I could continue my work for another two months, since I was authorized in Cuba to be in Mexico for two months, although the yearly contract had been interrupted for seven months. He was comfortably sitting in his chair congratulating me for the return, and right away handed me a document to be signed. He added that I did not have to sign it, but that it would be better if I did.

My face expressed confusion and surprise, especially for the way in which his eyes were staring at me. I sat down and read the two pages of the document. It stated that I had been working during the seven months I was held in Cuba, and it required my signature. This was false! One part of me was grateful to him for his role in helping my return. I could pay him with work but not by signing a false document. I gave the document back to him, looking at his face and explicitly rejecting his request. I excused myself and went back to where my students were waiting for me. Gladys was deeply impacted with the request and completely supported my response.

Since my arrival in Mexico, the two of us were doing all we could to continue working in Mexico. But to no avail. We had decided not to return to our native country. Finally, Gladys accepted the option knocking at the door of the American Consulate in Merida. In those two months after our interview in his office, I never saw my Mexican boss again. He completely ignored us. It was frustrating to see my boss' dignity falling down in our appreciation for him, but we felt peace in our hearts and minds because we had done the right thing. Gladys' bravery, principles, and values were transcendental, not only for getting together in Mexico, but also for staying united to face uncertainty in America.

# CHAPTER V -
## HER EXTRAORDINARY
## HUMAN RELATIONS

How wonderful it is to remember pleasant moments! One can comfortably sit down, close one's eyes, and travel in time. Sometimes one can listen to romantic musical pieces and rejoice, thinking about unforgettable memories. I keep so many good remembrances along the forty years we shared. One of them was our lengthy and interesting conversations. In reality, Gladys was an expert in oral communication. She had mastered Spanish, using the right words in the adequate context and circumstances. Her intelligence expanded in different dimensions from political topics to economic and social issues. Her brightest strength, though, was in interpersonal relations.

She could tap into people's souls by analyzing their behavior, the brilliance of their eyes, the way they smiled, the movement of the hands, their levels of attention, and the speed in which they answered questions. Gladys also had extensive capabilities for observation. I became acquainted with the range of her sensitive skills when we talked about certain events, of which I had not been aware, such as the absence of somebody in a place where he/she was expected to be. When listening to somebody about a given event, she could notice whether the person might be speaking the truth. Whenever we met a new individual and she told me that he appeared to be honest, most likely that would indeed be the case.

I could trust her judgment although at times she did not have solid arguments to prove it. I remembered that in the last book signing of *Havana-Merida-Chicago* in 2007, one perspective buyer approached me with an invitation to accompany him to meet a group of friends to promote the book.

While we were in the process of boarding the car, she confidentially told me that she felt the presence of a dangerous situation and did not want to leave me alone. There was only one seat available in his car, but Gladys insisted on being part of the group.

Some minutes after starting the car, the host of the invitation commented that, being an illegal immigrant in the US, he had been able to be clean for some months after being addicted to alcohol in his native country and added that America was a great country. Gladys stared at me, crunching her forehead, and pinched me. Some minutes later, the car stopped in an area close to a mall. She was somewhat shaky and holding my left arm. When we descended, she let everybody know that she suddenly was feeling bad. Being diabetic, she probably had a drop in her level of blood sugar. Our hosts tried to be helpful, but we preferred to go back home. Then they let us go. After a while, we boarded a bus going downtown, and later we rented a taxi cab.

She commented to me that something inside her was pressing to leaving the group. She felt that there was some possible danger at stake. We never saw those people again.

In her judgment of human mistakes, she always tried to find the reason behind the behavior. She did not coldly judge people without getting to know more about the situation, unless the issue related to beating a woman, a child, or people unable to defend themselves. She exuded sympathy, understanding, empathy, and sometimes even support, to homeless people who she insisted were not in a position to harm us.

An interesting anecdote took place when we were living in Humboldt Park, generally considered to be a dangerous zone rife with gangs in Chicago. One afternoon, we were in our way to board a bus in Division Street. A small group of young men were smoking and talking at the end of the same block, very close to the bus stop. Apparently something illegal was being done down there. Gladys took my hand and asked me in low voice to immediately go across the street without directly staring at the group. We kept walking faster but not running. When we got across the street from the bus stop, we continued walking for about half a block, waiting for the bus. Some minutes later, the bus was in sight, and the two of us walked somewhat faster to coincide with the bus arrival. The men were still smoking and talking. Gladys continued asking me not to make eye contact because that action might incite them to negatively react.

The arrival of the bus at the stop was simultaneous with our arrival. Nobody else was waiting for the bus, but a lady got off, and almost simultaneously we were placing our tokens in the driver's box— during our stay at the shelter, we were receiving tokens to pay for our transportation in the city.

While my wife was always alert to her surroundings in the neighborhood, she felt sorry for the drug addicts whose lives had been harmed by unfortunate childhoods, single mothers, and physical and sexual abuse. They deserved compassion, but nonetheless we had to be on the alert when they were closer to us.

To the woman in my life, it was hard to justify lies. She could easily realize when somebody was telling a lie.

She was able to evoke appreciation from a teacher, a student, a medical consultant, or an associate in a department store. When people who had met her heard that she had passed away, they almost immediately expressed condolences, commenting that Gladys was a real lady, always kind, friendly, and loving. Wherever she arrived, she scattered greetings and love all over the place, even at the nursing home where she died.

Gladys rejected a servile attitude toward bosses or persons of authority. She respectfully and kindly dealt with everybody, especially blue-collar workers, wherever we stayed in Cuba, Mexico, or the United States. She almost always elicited respect and admiration from everyone meeting her.

When we were in Mexico for a short time, she was voluntarily offering math classes to a department store associate, whom she frequently met while commuting from our home to the university. One day Gladys was looking at and touching some blouses on the sidewalk of a store, and a young associate—Carmen—approached her. After listening to Gladys' accent, Carmen asked where she came from and what she was doing in Merida. Having learned that my wife was teaching math, Carmen told her that she was preparing herself for a promotion in the store and that her mathematical background was not strong. Gladys agreed to help her. Upon getting the promotion, Carmen gave her a Guadalupe Virgin statuette.

If the reader is acquainted with my book *Havana-Merida-Chicago (A Journey to Freedom)*, he/she might remember the Mexican airport scene (shortly before boarding the flight to Chicago) when a virgin statuette inspired the custom official to let us board the plane.

It is hard to forget those stressful moments when the official was seated at his desk, browsing and confronting our documents and letters written by the Mexican custom authorities in Merida while the two of us were staring at each other in awe until the man noticed the statuette Gladys was holding in her arms. He then stood up, placed the documents in a drawer, and urged us to reach the gate that was about to be closed. We were the last passengers to board the plane! The same statuette has been sitting in the living room of our home for more than twenty years. It is a symbol of Gladys' compassion to an almost unknown young lady, who expressed her gratitude by giving the Mexican people's most adored representation of religious faith.

Gladys manifested her kindness with words, her beautiful brown eyes, and spontaneous smiles. She was modest and – above all, had a deeply human touch. It was difficult for her to say "I'm sorry" to a beggar's request. She was able to be in the other person's shoes and thanked God for not placing her in the shameful situations she was witnessing.

We were in Merida shortly after the signing of the North American Free Trade Agreement between Mexico, Canada, and the US. Quite a number of Yucatecan farmers went bankrupt by the competition with American exporters, and some of them migrated to the capital. In Merida's downtown, one could see many Mayan female farmers accompanied by barefoot children asking for alms.

Gladys suffered when she saw dirty children with weeping eyes asking for money. She just couldn't help but give them some. On many occasions, I was impacted by the loving scenes and had to pull her out on our way to the university. It was just impossible not to hug and kiss her after that humanitarian gesture. Then we went on our way to the bus stop.

Another example of her loving attitude was her relations with family. She deeply loved her parents, grandparents, siblings, uncles, cousins, and in-laws. Despite being a divorced marriage's child—raised by her grandfather's family, which was quite large—she always felt close to her parents. That was a home full of love, respect, and consideration. Money was an indispensable means to live but not the main reason for living. When any of the family members was facing an unfortunate situation, he/she would always find support and help at home. The woman in my life inherited all of her family's conduct and principles and adhered to them at all times.

Women's attraction to stores is much stronger than men's. It was hard for me to share her passion for shopping, but I had to accompany her as a translator, especially in our first year in the US. One of her frequent actions—hard to understand by me—was that she stayed a couple of hours looking for a pair of shoes and instead came out with a blouse and a skirt in her hands! During our first year in the US, we always had to be together because she needed a translator. I always admired how familiarly she related to the associates; I don't know how she could do that! If she visited a store more than once, she already knew the associates' names, asked about their children and their health, and her final good-bye was accompanied by a hug and some kisses close to the saleswomen's cheeks—a very familiar way women kiss their female acquaintances.

The same situation took place whenever we had doctor's visits when she greeted and kissed the nurses and laboratory assistants and cordially welcomed the physicians. Our weekly participation in mass always ended in the same fashion, especially in kissing and holding the parishioners' children, who were very special for her, as the reader will learn in the following chapter. I wondered, was there any limit to her capacity for loving human beings?

# CHAPTER VI -
# HER LOVE AND IDENTIFICATION WITH CHILDREN

Gladys got pregnant on five occasions; however, she could never become a mother due to the capacity of her uterus to expand—it did not expand when the fetus grew to a certain level, and she had spontaneous miscarriages after the third, fourth, or fifth months. As any woman deeply in love with the man in her life, she eagerly wanted to give me a child. In the last pregnancy, she was prescribed bed rest for five months, but the miscarriage happened anyway. On this occasion, we were closer than ever. We both grieved the loss, as well as the conclusion that her motherhood could never take place. On one hand, our relationship was very strong and kept growing, but on the other hand, frustration enhanced her love for children.

From my first marriage, I had two children, whom she wanted to get closer to and to deserve love from. Regardless of Gladys' sincere attempts to gain their appreciation, she could never "tear down the wall" between my children and her. As I previously noted, she did not have anything to do with my divorce; nevertheless, my children rejected her. It appeared as if my happiness with the woman in my life was not accepted by my children.

The following is an anecdote showing my children's animosity toward my wife, whose only crime was to make me happy, contrasting with the unfortunate marriage in which—paradoxically—they had been born.

During the summer of 1993, I was seriously ill, diagnosed with pneumonia due to lack of food and excessive amount of work. At this time Cuba was going through what is known as the Special Period, which led to scarcity of staples and medicines in the country. My children knew of my sickness, but they never showed up to check on me.

One of these summer days, Gladys met Tonito, my son, on her way to the market. At the time, he was twenty-seven years old and was riding a bike. She approached my son, asking about his health and the reasons for being so close to our home. Tonito informed her that he was going to the diplo market with the intention to buy a cake for his mother's birthday. As a result of the Soviet Union's collapse, the economic situation in Cuba was so dire that it was difficult to buy a cake in the domestic market in Cuban pesos. A cake could only be bought for children celebrating up to seven years of age. My children had access to US dollars and could afford to buy a cake in the diplo market.

Gladys asked my son if he was going to see me since he was so close to my home and knew that I was sick. He answered that he was in a hurry and did not have time to visit me. She then grabbed the bike, letting him know that she would return it as soon as he returned from visiting me. She was ready to wait for his return right there. Grudgingly Tonito looked at her. There were no comments, only a silent interchange of glances. He started to walk toward my home.

I was lying down when I heard a knocking at the door. I opened the door and was pleasantly surprised to see my son. Noting that Tonito was somewhat embarrassed, I asked my son about his health and then why he had delayed so long before coming to see me. Tonito was not talkative but instead silent and worried. Looking into his eyes, I asked him why he had come to see me. My son explained that Gladys had obliged him to go there and taken his bike to make sure that he was coming to see me. It was obvious that my son was not worried about my health. Therefore, I thanked him for his visit and told him to go back to recover his bike. Tonito's face immediately changed from sadness to happiness; he kissed my forehead and ran downstairs to recover his bike.

My children never reciprocated Gladys' loving attitude to them, and I felt that they did not love me either. There was a wall of resentment, envy, and hatred between my children and the couple I was a part of. However, my wife appreciated them and never stopped loving children, especially the little ones. In her view, almost all children were lovely.

As soon as Gladys noticed a little angel's presence, she approached and asked about the child's name and commented about how cute the child was. At times, the child felt embarrassed by Gladys' loving welcome and hid behind the mother or father; but my wife insisted, and finally, the creature smiled at her.

When we attended church on Sunday mornings, there were five to ten children present. As soon as the mass was over, Gladys went to look for them, kissing and embracing them and asking how they were. She talked to them with a smile on her face. When talking to girls, she commented favorably about their clothes, shoes, and bows. When talking to boys, she praised that they were cute and little gentlemen dressed similarly to their fathers. She took many minutes in those lovely encounters while I was pressing her to go upstairs to the coffee hour. She bade them farewell with kisses.

Once we were upstairs at the coffee hour, she kept on approaching the children while I was talking to other parishioners. When I was looking at her attraction to children and the extensive farewells, I remembered our own extensive farewells in which we bade farewell several times before finally going on our way. The farewells were part of the rendezvous. To the little ones, Gladys showed the same love. Then there was the unforgettable scene which represents in itself the close connection and chemistry that existed between her and other children. After one doctor's visit, both of us were waiting for a bus at the nearest crossing. We had been waiting for some minutes when a school bus stopped just in front of us as a result of the change from yellow to red light.

The bus was full of infants. Gladys was looking at them with a loving smile on her face. Then—suddenly—she placed her right hand in the mouth and sent a kiss to one of the children. Immediately all children moved to the side of the bus closer to us and started to send kisses to her and wave their hands in a unanimous way. The scene was remarkably loving. All children wanted to express their love for Gladys. The traffic light changed to green, but the driver did not start the engine immediately. Apparently he had also been impacted by the unusually loving scene. The children and Gladys kept sending kisses and waving hands to each other.

I was flabbergasted. I had witnessed a very tender scene in which her love for children had elicited a loving reaction from many infants. I couldn't help embracing her and telling her how much I loved her. It was as if the children had been impacted by the presence of an angel. Delving deeper in Gladys' expression of love, the following chapter will deal with the diverse forms in which she manifested love for me.

# CHAPTER VII -
# THE DIVERSE WAYS OF EXPRESSING LOVE FOR HER MAN

Gladys possessed a superior intellectual capacity. She had a special knack for creating and keeping alive the flame of our love. If we had been alive for another twenty years, most likely we would have completed our sixtieth wedding anniversary. One anecdote that exemplifies the former assumption is one of Gladys' answers to a question posed by a physical therapist that was treating her. He commented that we appeared to be in a very close relationship and asked her how many married years we had completed so far. With a smile on her face and looking eye to eye with the therapist, she immediately answered that, had she been given the opportunity to have more than one life, she would definitely marry me again. We were convinced that we were meant to be together. By remembering and analyzing our wonderful married life, I can clearly distinguish at least seven different ways through which our love relationship was consolidated.

1. *Our skills and weaknesses complemented each other.* It is interesting to note that the two of us constituted an integral body of complementary dexterities. I felt almost unable to carry out the activities which she could perform relatively easily; conversely, the activities which were easily accomplished by me were very hard for her. Let us take some examples: A) I had the strength and drive to optimistically

and promptly undertake new tasks, while she was more objective and careful, calling my attention to the possible difficulties I had not foreseen in my enthusiasm. B) She was very analytical and, in a brief time, able to observe most people's fundamental characteristics such as honesty and sincerity. It was harder for me to capture another person's body language and subtle expressions. C) It was easy for me to orient myself geographically speaking, whereas it was difficult for Gladys to know whether she was going south or north. D) My wife was very patient to handle computer prompts and to discover their whereabouts and secrets, while I was impatient and requested her help when suddenly surprised by an unexpected new window when pressing a key on the keyboard. E) She was able to successfully follow written instructions contained in a brochure to install a printer, and I felt frustrated when all of a sudden there was no sound from the computer or an unexpected prompt spoiled part of my work, and I had to look for a brochure with instructions. F) When I lost my temper and became angry or aggravated, she was like a tranquilizer that calmed me down. G) She helped me to be more diplomatic during confrontations or arguments while I pushed her when she felt insecure. Our love got stronger when we celebrated our mutual differences and compromised them to resolve issues.

2. *The simultaneous combination of protecting and being protected by, me.* She was very concerned about my health. She did everything in her power to make me aware of the possible risks of getting a cold, not visiting the doctor's office on time whenever some apparently small discomfort was discovered, eating food not well cooked, or walking too fast and running into obstacles due to the pressures of stress. At the same time, she needed to feel protected in my arms and also in relation to financial issues. Often, she commented to me that she felt so protected being held in my arms. With her beautiful eyes and voice she was telling me how her love

for me was enhanced each time she felt my protection. I felt the need to protect her, to defend her against all physical or emotional enemies. This mutual feeling of protection was sublime; it was the very communion of our souls.

3. *The simultaneous combination of loving me unconditionally and of claiming my respect and consideration for her.* She clearly showed me her unconditional love on several occasions, such as A) when we did not have a home of our own and had to live in somebody else's home without having real privacy. During several months, we had to hire rooms in hotels or motels in order to enjoy our love relationship under more favorable circumstances. B) When we simultaneously were deceived by Castro communism's utopia and could not bear the indoctrination through the media and had not yet found the possibility of leaving the country. C) When we escaped from communism and had to start from scratch in Mexico and the United States. D) When we faced financial issues due to maintaining my children's alimony beyond the time required by law and facing innumerable mechanical problems and expenditures with my Polsky Fiat due to lack of parts from Poland. E) When Gladys (being forty-eight years old) contacted the American Consulate in Merida as a unique available possibility of not returning to Cuba, in order to live in the US without knowing English to accompany me in the adventure of starting a new and uncertain life. E) When, during our first five months in Chicago, we were living in a shelter at Humboldt Park, a neighborhood at the time experiencing serious security problems in related to gangs and shootings. Her commitment to our love was always the same, regardless of our economic, political, or social situations. She loved me because of who I was, not because of my material possessions.

Nonetheless, at the same time, when I was sometimes overwhelmed by financial issues or influenced by my successes in my professional life, I did not treat her as she deserved; she called my attention to the fact that I should not confuse her love for me with submission to my tantrums. She sat down with me, staring in my eyes in a very serious and solemn way, and demanded my respect. Regardless of how nervous or stressed I might be due to intense work teaching at different institutions or self-centeredness due to good results in my career, she never accepted my raising my voice or talking to her in a disrespectful way. I had to respect her as my wife, somebody who loved me deeply, but who also loved and respected herself. I received a wakeup call and repented of my incorrect attitude. She always knew how to demand respect at the same time that she loved me deeply. Even when she was scolding me, I was able to feel her love. She was ready to let the man of her life go if he did not respect her. Her honorable and noble attitude made me love her more deeply and, as a result, try to be a better husband. She always was my companion, my advisor, the lady who took care of me with all of her love. Gladys deserved a husband able to behave as honorably and adequately as she did.

4. *Her capacity for exacting and forgiving.* She relentlessly tried to improve my multiple shortcomings in relating to other people, such as dressing adequately while teaching at the university or at the institutions where I was doing research. She reminded me of good manners while eating at restaurants or generally when addressing other people. She did not overlook any deficiency she had observed in my behavior; however, at the same time, she forgave me as soon as my attitude started to change. It is interesting to observe that when she saw that I was disappointed or frustrated but trying to overcome the difficulty, she placed her cheeks close to my lips and asked me to kiss and to embrace her. She knew that I was going to change and tried to find the best ways to obtain her objectives. By using this eminently feminine way—of combining scolds with love—the tense situation

was dissolved, and all the differences were resolved directly as soon as the problems were detected.

5. *The ability for holding an interesting, varied, and extensive conversation without any trace of boredom.* Gladys was a very intelligent woman. Professionally speaking, she finished her bachelor's degree in accounting with flying colors at the University of Havana and also two years of a bachelor's in chemistry at the Technological Institute Jose Antonio Echevarría. She worked as a financial specialist in several ministries in Cuba, as a faculty of mathematics at the Universidad Autónoma de Yucatan, Mexico, and a teacher of Spanish, the GED, and Introduction to Business in the United States.

She enjoyed reading world literature and had an inborn vocation for psychology. When we were dating, she gave me Victor Hugo's book *Les Misérables,* which helped me improve my tolerance for demanding perfection in other people. I could identify with Javert, the relentless persecutor of the hero of the novel, who had stolen a piece of bread from the window of a bakery.

She was highly cultured, which enabled her to talk about economics, the international political economy, finance, health issues, political trends in Europe, China, Latin America, and so on. We shared common political and religious standpoints. We enjoyed talking whenever possible. I never asked myself what topic would be analyzed with her.

The conversation flowed constantly and continuously. During our forty years, six months, and one day of togetherness, I don't remember ever feeling bored. Every now and then she asked me to "tell her a story" about my research papers or articles from *The Economist* or the *Financial Times.* She knew how to listen, how to ask, and how to answer questions. It actually was an interesting learning experience for both of us. On several occasions, she commented to me that our best moments took place simply when we were together, holding hands, immersed in our deep sentimental and loving identification.

6. *Her physical and intellectual support in moments of professional indetermination in Cuba.* In the 1980s when my colleagues at the College of Economics of the University of Havana tried to boycott the defense of my first dissertation, Gladys gave me the support that I badly needed. She attended the scientific session where my dissertation was rejected and shared in my frustration. When the activity was over, instead of talking about the refusal, she took me by the hand, and persuaded me to go to the beach. We started to walk barefoot in the sand. The warm waves of the sea were caressing our feet and gently pushing us. Our toes were covered by sand. We looked at each other. Little by little, stress was being relaxed. There was a moment when we exchanged kisses and started to sing. At that moment, we shook our feet, dried them with a towel she had brought, and were ready to go home. To breathe the pure air coming from the Caribbean Sea and to feel the breeze caressing our faces in combination with the songs helped us to weather the storm threatening my scientific future.

Gladys also helped me organize my work time because I had been addicted to overwork and also to accepting many research activities. When she realized that I was about to burst, she asked me to include extracurricular activities such as going to the movies. I had to learn how to prioritize my activities and to say no to some unforeseen tasks, which were not indispensable or even convenient to me.

During the first semester in 1993 an extraordinarily important event took place in our lives. Since the last quarter of 1991, I had been deceived by the Cuban political system. I felt a deep frustration because I could not help my country in the programming of the sugar crop to which I had dedicated twenty-five years of intense research during which the sugar industry was the vital industry of my country. On top of that, the collapse of the Soviet Union—which considerably worsened the Cuban economy so highly dependent on the Soviet economy—negatively impacted faculty motivation to teach and students' desire to learn.

My research team was dismantled due to lack of resources from the Ministry of Sugar and the University of Havana. I was convinced that neither pedagogically nor politically could I realize myself in Cuba. I had to leave the country. For more information, this author refers the readers to his book *Havana-Merida-Chicago (A Journey to Freedom)*.

In the context of the Ministry of Higher Education in Cuba's new policy related to sending Cuban professors to teach in Latin America universities, I saw the possibility of leaving my country and opening the possibility of realizing my intellectual and personal dreams. To be hired abroad was a respite and relief for the College of Economics faculty. The price was high because the faculty had to travel alone for a year and to contribute 75% of their income in foreign currency to the University of Havana. Anyway, at least, faculty could acquire regular products that had already disappeared from the Cuban market, and this hiring could help improve the standard of living at home.

I was the only PhD in Economics at the University of Havana who also held a doctorate in a science degree. My teaching career spanned thirty years. I worked for ten years as the leader of a research team. When the hiring of Cuban faculty started, I had sent letters to several foreign universities but had not received any answer. Anybody in my situation would feel aggravated and discouraged under the aforementioned circumstances.

Gladys knew of my conundrum and one morning sat down with me to talk about the issue. She held my hands firmly and inspired me to overcome the situation. I was not the optimistic man she was used to seeing, but—as always—she was the smiling girl with bright eyes staring lovingly at me. She started to talk about my experience in the sugar industry and asked me how important or interesting that research line would be for a Latin American university, even more so considering the unfavorable situation of the Cuban sugar industry. I nodded. She was starting to make me think about a new adventure.

My expression started to change from incredulous to hopeful. Gladys commented that in those days several international seminars and conferences were being held at the Cuban Palace of Conventions and the Cuban Academy of Sciences. The topic was environmental issues, of which I had no clue at the time. Then she asked me about the possibility of becoming a specialist in environmental economics. She held my hands even more tightly. She trusted my skills in learning subjects. At first I was hesitant, but I did not see any other possibility. She assured me that I could learn something about the topic and maybe initiate a career in that field. I trusted Gladys' common sense.

Sometimes we disagreed about certain issues and reality proved her right. When that happened I would stand up and embraced her tightly. She was somewhat surprised by my speedy reaction, but her face was gleaming with joy. This was the beginning of the new adventure.

One year and a half had gone by since our conversation. I had visited the Academy of Sciences and the Ministry of Sugar libraries and consulted agronomists at the Ministry of Sugar, who had a wide experience with the damage that the sugar industry had done to agriculture. I prepared three papers related to the environmental damage done by the sugar industry derivatives (especially paper industry using bagasse—a byproduct of the sugar cane) to the production of fish and shrimp because the rivers going to their habitats were polluted and had affected them. I had the papers published in a journal regarding the sugar industry and kept the College of Economics informed of my scientific activity.

On one of those days, I received an urgent message from the College of Economics Dean. I was seated in the Dean's reception office waiting, while the assistant offered me a cup of coffee. Normally I do not drink coffee, but to have said no would have been considered to be rude.

After a while, a smiling young man invited me to come into his office. He shook my hand and congratulated me. He asked me if I had any idea of the reason for the meeting, and I said no. He then let me know that the college had received a request from a university in Mexico for a doctor in economics and specialist in environmental economics. With a smile on his face, he asked me if I would be interested in working in Mexico for a year without my wife and contributing 75% of my salary to the university.

I happened to be the only professor at the college with experience in environmental economics. My eyes were shining and reflected happiness. He simply hugged and congratulated me. The Communist Party had already approved my one year teaching in Mexico. The Dean was a man of about 5'3" and a nice person. He told me that the contract would start in six weeks. Anybody in my case could not wait to see his wife and to be on his way to see her.

Gladys was waiting for me at the balcony. She had seen me coming from the bus stop. Some minutes later, she was standing at the door with her arms extended to me. With a big smile on my face I could only tell her,

—We did it. In two months I shall start a one-year contract in Mexico thanks to you.

7. *The reiterated salvation of my life.* On several occasions, my wife actively participated in helping me evade death.

   a. *My flare-up in the sacro-lumbar zone of my spinal vertebrae.* During the last months of 1992, I felt an acute pain around my waist. I could hardly walk and had to lie in bed for some weeks. The pain was severe. It was necessary to have a shot in the spinal column directly on the bone. The closest orthopedic hospital was located four kilometers from home. Transportation was—and still is—a serious problem in Havana. It was necessary to walk four blocks to get to the bus stop and to board two buses. Taxis were only available at the hospitals and were only for individuals with access to dollars: we were not members of this select group of Cubans at the time. Another possible way to solve this problem would be to ask for a ride. In our building, there were three families who owned a car, but gasoline was seriously rationed and was used only for the needs of the family.

   The pain in my back became extremely acute after the first two weeks. Gladys decided to take me to the hospital. We knew that at the hospital they had the badly-needed shot of prednisone. With her help, I descended the five floors walking on one foot and holding the handrails. With great courage, Gladys supported me to stand on one foot. After a while, we arrived to the cross where the buses were circulating. There was a line of five people in front of us. The first bus came after ten or fifteen minutes, but only the five people could get into the bus. While I was seated on a bench, my wife was approaching cars that stopped at the traffic light. After a while, one kind-hearted driver agreed to take us to the hospital.

Once at the emergency room of the hospital, I was placed in a wheelchair and transferred to a room where I received the shot. A few seconds later, the pain began to recede. The nurses also gave me some painkillers. The return trip home was much better. We only had to wait about an hour to board a taxi accompanied by two other patients. The taxi stopped just in front of our building, and I could ascend the staircase on my own. Without Gladys, it would have been impossible to get to the hospital.

b.  *Pneumonia that seriously threatened my life.* In the spring of 1993, shortly before going to Mexico, I arrived home one day feeling seriously ill with high fever. I was shivering and constantly coughing.

I had just had a doctor's appointment at the Calixto Garcia Hospital in Havana, close to the university. With the use of the stethoscope— the X-ray equipment was not working at the hospital—the physician discovered that I had a serious infection of pneumonia. On top of that there were no antibiotics available, neither at the hospital, nor at the local drugstores. I'd had a serious pneumonia attack, and I needed to rest and to eat as much as possible.

Just imagine Cuba during the Special Period: scarce electricity, food, and medicines. At home, we had very little food and the only medicine available was aspirin. In order to reduce my fever, Gladys took my clothes off and gave me a bath in cold water together with an alcohol rub. My fever went down from 40 to 38 centigrade degrees (approximately 103 to 100 Fahrenheit degrees), but I still felt very weak.

She went to visit some neighbors who had access to dollars to ask for food, and received two drumsticks and a piece of chicken breast from a neighbor who saw her crying in desperation because she thought that I was about to die. After having chicken soup, I got slightly better. Gladys went to see her family in Menocal and a cousin who worked as butcher, Ramoncito. She also called my mother who brought a branch of bananas she had grown in her backyard. I needed additional protein.

The only possibility was to buy meat from small farmers—at the time the farmer's market was prohibited by Fidel Castro—but Gladys had received some news about a farmer supplying meat. After a four-hour absence, my wife returned with several pounds of pork. As a result of this extra food and the alcohol rub, she could reduce the fever and was able to save my life without medicines.

c. *My involuntary arrival to a hospital in Chicago while I was having a heart attack.* From 1996 to 1998, both of us led very active working lives. I was working in one university and two colleges besides working as a freelancer translating from English to Spanish. Gladys was studying English intensively and teaching Spanish as a freelancer. The stress was considerable for both of us.

For the first two weeks in September 1998, I was experiencing some sort of pressure or discomfort in my chest, which appeared to be due to heartburn. On September 19, the pain increased, and Gladys obliged me to go to the closest emergency room. When the taxi arrived at the hospital, I was excusing myself to the physicians for the "unnecessary" inconvenience. After the first exam, the physicians told me that I was having a heart attack. Then I was really afraid and was immediately taken to the hospital area for heart problems. My wife was crying incessantly and called our spiritual father because we thought that I needed the extreme unction. Reverend Morales arrived immediately and found Gladys crying desperately, asking the Lord to take her instead of me.

At the hospital, she was beside me and asked the nurses which were the symptoms or the numbers in the boards that would elicit immediate action. At the first sign of urgency, she ran for the nurse, brought her to the room and showed the numbers. The danger was immediate. The cardiologist would be there in less than half an hour.

While I was being transferred in the stretcher to the operating room, Gladys was crying desperately. Silently and with a smile on my face, I prayed and thanked the Lord for His blessings—my exceptional wife, incredible mother, scholarly career, students in Cuba, Mexico, and the United States, books, and children—and commended myself to Him. When waking up from the anesthesia, I could only see a mist. I was surprised to be alive.

Here is an incredible example of Gladys' commitment to me. She was seated by my side in the room. My wife received instructions not to let me touch the wound in my groin until it was healed. Being unconscious, there was a risk that I might involuntarily touch it. I had been given an angioplasty with a stent in the central artery of my heart. Gladys was beside me all the time without sleeping or eating for four days, taking care of my groin and looking at the numbers on the board. After that time, the cardiologist told her of my survival of the heart attack. Then she fainted. The doctor told me that she was stressed without any heart problem. I did not know how to compensate her for so much love, so much care, and so much dedication. When I asked her, she only said with a smile on her face and watery eyes,

—The best reward I can have is that you are alive.

# CHAPTER VIII -
# HER EXEMPLARY MODESTY

Since our very first encounter, I could feel that Gladys was a modest woman. As time went by, my initial impression was confirmed and proven right.

Let me describe Gladys as a woman from an external standpoint, starting with the way she dressed. Just imagine a woman with a minimum amount of make-up with perfectly traced red lipstick and a simple touch of make-up on her eyelids and cheeks. Her shape was ideal for a sculptor and her dresses perfectly fitted a slender silhouette. Her face was a nice combination of brown eyes with a slightly Asian appearance, a moderately flat nose typical of African ancestry, and a perfectly good sized pair of lips characteristic of European roots. Her face was wrinkle-free, even after sixty-seven birthdays. Her skin was taut. Her voice had the same soft and melodious tone of a soap opera actress in her first role. She did not have to modulate her voice because it was naturally perfect and deeply feminine. Her dresses, skirts, and blouses were done by an expert seamstress, who was considered to be part of the family. Gladys was a very feminine lady, even when she was wearing pants—a good representation of a typically Cuban girl! A male reader can easily imagine the impact that my wife made on me from an external point of view. I was bewitched—but neither bothered nor bewildered—and simply astonished at the contemplation of such external beauty.

Besides her impressive external qualities, from the very first day, I could feel that she also possessed internal fascination, adorableness, and loveliness. On top of physical attractiveness, during our forty years together I never witnessed her boasting about her beauty or saw that she felt herself above other ladies. She never spoke about her natural good looks—in comparison with other women—but rather as a gift of God or inheritance from her mother, who simultaneously was beautiful and discreet. When choosing a necklace, earrings, watch, or ring, she always preferred the least luxurious. She did not like to call society's attention to what she wore. Gladys was very careful of measuring the amount of make-up, the discreetness of her clothes, and did not have a single piece of clothes considered to be provocative to men. Presumption was never one of her personal characteristics. After our first night together, I could testify about the advantages of a woman being modest in her make up. The lady I met in my bed in the early morning was the same that I had seen in the evening.

The woman in my life was raised by her aunts, delicate ladies, who knew how to dress adequately and were dressmakers for El Encanto, the most exclusive department store in Havana before the revolution. At home, where she stayed from birth until her first marriage, there were no luxurious articles though the house was always kept impeccably clean. The numerous family members were raised with good manners, solid moral values, a cordial treatment for visitors, hospitality, and modesty. Her grandparents raised a family under the principles of love, respect, and consideration, as well as honesty and morality.

The head of the family was the owner of a medium-sized farm, a veteran in the war against Spain. In that home everybody observed the rules of formal education. No scandals, high tones, or rude voices were typically heard. There were discussions but very few arguments, which were carried out in a respectful way. The family financially supported their "granddaughter–niece" to complete primary and secondary education until her sixteenth birthday. Then, she started to work eight hours per day and to simultaneously study for high school, and later on, for her baccalaureate degree in the evenings. In summary, Gladys was raised in a home where work and study were considered to be the best ways to make a living in a moral and mutually respectful context.

Ever since my wife was a little girl, she showed pedagogic skill by helping classmates and collaborating with the teacher, who became her inspiration and the ideal version of an instructor. Gladys had a developed a conception about a teacher's role in the students' intellectual formation by trying to foster reasoning skills rather than memorization.

In Cuba, her professional work developed in the financial-economic industry up to August 1994, when she arrived in Yucatan, Mexico to work as faculty in mathematics at the Autonomous University of Yucatan, where she was hired for two academic years. During those years, she gained the students' respect and appreciation because of both her innate pedagogic skills and kindness. She was able to inspire students and to get the best of them in the classroom.

There was a special student who was reluctant to study mathematics but who was inspired by Gladys in such a way that he became one of the best students in the class. He was the son of a senator in the Mexican government. Despite the constant praise received by Gladys for her successful performance in Mexico she never lost her modesty, which elicited an ever-larger admiration. My wife felt blessed by, and grateful to, the Lord for giving her the possibility of teaching in a new country.

One of the most outstanding of Gladys' virtues was the kindness and sweetness she systematically expressed in her relations with all human beings she encountered everywhere.

Some months ago, I was speaking with Gladys about the possibility of my retirement from DePaul University after more than fifty years of my continuous teaching career in Cuba, Mexico, and the U.S.

To my surprise, she looked at me in a strange way, with a gloomy and somewhat sad face. Her eyes were not shining, but somber. I immediately approached her quietly, asking the reason for the unexpected reaction to my comment.

She answered that she had just realized that her life had not been relevant to anybody while I had been successful scholarly and pedagogically. I immediately expressed my disapproval with her unfair self-evaluation and comparison. In Cuba, women did not have the same opportunities as men. Had it not been for my mother's idea of obliging me to study English before finishing high school, I would not have given the scholarship to go to Scotland. I worked hard, but I was also very lucky to find the right people at the right time.

She never had the opportunity of teaching at the University of Havana; therefore, her possibilities of holding a PhD were impossible in the industry where she was working. She was a very smart woman with a huge capacity for learning and possessed noticeable common sense, which in reality is the least common of the senses. Thanks to her I was alive, and we could leave Cuba for good! She had intelligently transformed me into a better human being.

Gladys insisted on diminishing her importance and finally she had to admit that she had been an indispensable support in my career. She had forgotten the dozens of Mexican students who were blessed by having her as a mathematics instructor and the hundreds of Hispanic students who attended St. Augustine College and were immensely helped to build business plans and become owners of their own businesses. She had kept many lives away from dangerous activities.

But more than that, her human nature was excellent and recognized by almost everyone she met. And what about children? Infants were always attracted to her kindness. For them, Gladys was somebody very special, a kind of angel who was always smiling at them.

On a personal note, I felt very little in relation to her greatness. When my wife was fighting against my egoism and personality problems, for which I had been rejected by some people, she was encouraging me to overcome my deficiencies. She was the only woman who preferred to make me angry by fighting against my ego and, by arguing with her, improve my behavior.

She immediately rejected any arrogance or conceit. She felt hurt when witnessing or knowing of an abuse against children, women, or even defenseless men. She was able to feel anybody's pain as if it were her own. She was always ready to give a hand to anybody in need or in disgrace without taking into consideration negative consequences that she might experience as a result of the helpful gesture. She never hated anyone, even if he/she wanted to hurt her.

Gladys' modesty was an obstacle to recognizing her own good qualities. Few people are able to be in other persons' shoes and to apply the commandment "Thou should love thy neighbor as thyself." Gladys followed Christian behavior and inspired other people to behave generously. My wife was so great and modest that she could not see her own greatness. I witnessed the impact of her kindness and love to so many people when they knew of her decease. All physicians, nurses, students, and friends coincided in recognizing her kindness. The woman in my life was an extremely modest, kind, and human lady. Gladys' death was a loss to anybody lucky enough to have met her.

I learned from my wife during our forty years together. She had many virtues and qualities that I discovered with the passing of time and the emergence of difficulties. Nonetheless, my greatest surprise took place when I witnessed the lesson of courage, kindness, and firmness she gave me during the last year of her life. The next chapter will deal with this exemplary phase of a fruitful life.

# CHAPTER IX -
# THE EXTRAORDINARY WAY IN
# WHICH SHE FACED DEATH

Generally speaking, Gladys and I enjoyed relatively good health considering our ages, At the end of 2009, though, we received a wake-up call when both of us experienced blocked arteries. In 2005, her primary care physician detected some shadows in an X-ray. They were discarded as being non-cancerous and did not appear to be a sign of something worse. As a matter of fact, the later prognosis was pulmonary stiffness, which makes it harder for the patients to exhale air from their lungs. Neither of us, nor some of the doctors we consulted, had a clear idea of the causes of the disease.

At first, we thought that her smoking habit had been the cause of the disease, but according to some specialists' experiences, smoking was not necessarily a cause of pulmonary stiffness. The sickness is not widely known, but after some months, we *learned* that it was incurable. In fact, we met the best pulmonary specialists at Northwestern Memorial Hospital, but by then it was too late for Gladys. Her sickness had considerably advanced.

The initial symptoms appeared in 2014. She then experienced respiratory deficiencies whenever she walked fast or ran after eating. By then the shadows discovered in her lungs had grown slightly larger, but it was not deemed necessary to do further testing. On two occasions, we asked her lung specialist if she could travel abroad, and the answer was yes.

We were not lucky enough to meet the right specialists in 2014. In the fall, we were traveling in the city of Toledo, Spain, and Gladys could not ascend even a mid-size elevation. We had to separate ourselves from the group because she could not continue. One month later, we were on a Mediterranean cruise, and in both Greece and Italy she could not participate in some off-shore excursions, which implied long walking periods. Then we made the decision not to travel again unless her condition improved.

From that moment onward, it was necessary to pay closer attention to her sickness and to look for the best specialists. From March to October 2015, she was hospitalized on three occasions and stayed in a nursing home twice. During those months, she had to undergo painful laboratory tests and medical procedures. She was prescribed a newly approved medicine that was supposed to stop her malaise from worsening, but she had to stop two months after starting, because it was damaging her digestive system.

From her first hospitalization, we learned that her only chance of survival would be to receive a lung transplant, which had a very low probability of success given Gladys' age and the small likelihood of finding a donor. She also was expected to lose twenty pounds during a relatively short time. During her second hospitalization, she experienced an apparent improvement by being administered a medicine that adversely affected her diabetes. One of the worst parts of the process she was going through was that she had to be seated upright in order to sleep, otherwise her oxygen level would drop.

These adverse circumstances had an incredibly positive effect on our love relationship. We were together each and every day that she was hospitalized or in the nursing home. In her individual hospital room, Gladys was connected to a compressor. She was alone and checking her watch, seated in an inclinable bed with a finger introduced into an oximeter. Her thoughts were away from the room. She was serious, and at times, a smile appeared on her face, probably when remembering happy moments with the man in her life.

There was a knock on her door, and a nurse entered the room with a couple of syringes. After the nurse finished drawing blood, Gladys lay back. Her face was not sad, but attentive to the watch, the oximeter, and the door. There was another knock on the door. I arrived with a smile on my face and kissed Gladys right away. Our hands intertwined. Gladys' face was radiant. I was also happy, but my eyes also reflected worry. I saw her every day and stayed close to her for several hours, paying attention to her needs. I felt that there was not much time available for our togetherness. My eyes showed lack of sleep.

Gladys appeared to be encouraging me and was smiling. She looked beautiful although her hair was 50% black and 50% white. I stayed with her for five or six hours, but it was already time to return home. My wife was hospitalized in the southeast of Chicago, and our home was located in the northeast. I had to get a taxi, but, at the hospital, taxis were not easily available after 6 p.m. Our farewell was tender as always, with promises to come back the following day.

The moments before I returned home were also very special, accompanied with kisses and hugs. It was hard to hug her because she was seated on the bed. Our romantic glances went on and on. She repeatedly told me how much she loved me. She did not want me to be sad, and I had to force myself to restrain my tears in front of her. She never cried or complained about her weak health when I was present. We pressed our lips together, and I slowly left the room, looking backward two or three times.

I boarded a taxi, ready for the long distance, a twenty-minute ride. I opened the window, and a draft of fresh air slapped my watery eyes. It was very hard for me to accept that soon this extraordinary marriage would be definitely over. To remember the respiratory masks and tubes in her face impacted me deeply. How could I live without her?

After two hospitalizations and one stay in a nursing home, Gladys experienced an improvement, and for three weeks we were together at last at home. Every night we enjoyed intimate moments that were unforgettable.

I never missed a class during the months that Gladys was sick. I had classes from Monday to Thursday. We had to sleep in separate places. When going to bed, I was really exhausted especially due to the stress of seeing her connected to two compressors (one in our bedroom and another one in the living room). Almost every night around eleven o'clock, she walked slowly towards my bed, stopping frequently to catch her breath, and then she sat beside me. Her face was so beautiful. She was smiling. She caressed my arms and my face. We were like youngsters in love.

After a while, I inclined myself towards her and hugged her. Our embrace was warm and we remained silent. She stayed like that around half an hour. Then, as sweetly as I could, I told her about my need to fall asleep. Then she slowly stood up to return to the living room where she had better conditions to sleep herself. She was looking at me as if she were a young girl watching her first boyfriend and slowly closed the door.

When I had classes at noon, as soon as I woke up, I would lay beside her, embracing, kissing, and singing to her. She remained quiet, and then she fell asleep in my arms. These minutes, which appeared to be seconds, were the happiest times we spent together. It was as if she was not sick at all and the world was contained in us. There were no problems to be worried about. It was just us together in our intimacy.

When we were so close, every now and then I could not avoid some tears. When she realized that I was sad, she asked me to smile and to enjoy those moments.

There is an interesting anecdote that took place just two days before her death. She wanted to talk to her cousin, who is almost the only survivor of her family in Cuba. Clarita's voice appeared to be emotional, and then Gladys—showing another bright point in her marvelous personality—asked her not to cry because she was ready and happy to see the family she had not seen for many years.

Gladys' comment made us all laugh. She was able to break the stress of those moments, and all she wanted was to listen to her cousin's voice for the last time. After that moment, they started talking about funny situations and laughing. That was the last possible moment that the call could have happened, because Gladys' health worsened soon thereafter. She was connected to a bigger mask that would not allow her to talk over the phone.

She was telling me that I had made her a happy woman for forty years and that I did not have the right to cry. Her only worry was over who would take care of me. She wanted me to get a new girlfriend.

On October 6, I taught in the morning and told the nurse that, if Gladys condition worsened, he should call me right away because I wanted to accompany her in her last moments. Just as soon as I finished teaching and went to my office, the nurse called me urging me to go to the nursing home.

When I arrived at her room, Gladys was still alive but in agony. She was simultaneously connected to two strong compressors of pure oxygen. Nonetheless, her oximeter did not go beyond 80, and 89 was the number at which her lungs could no longer transmit oxygen to her brain. For two hours, I tried to feed her, to lower the room temperature to the minimum because she was sweating intensely. Then I started to embrace, kiss, and even sing to her.

In her agonizing broken voice she was able to tell me how much she loved me. Making an extraordinary effort she told me,

—Antonio, now you are a diamond.

Soon afterwards, she stopped babbling, her eyes turned blank, and her head fell backwards. She had died in my arms. I could not help sobbing strongly and felt as if I had thunder inside my mouth. At least she stopped suffering.

All the time I was waiting for the cremation personnel to pick up her body, I was beside her. She was so lovely. Her face reflected peace. I kissed her so many times, but I did not cry. She appeared to be sleeping. She was beautiful until the last moment of her life.

It is not possible to finish this chapter without emphasizing Gladys' stoicism during the process of her physical suffering growing more severe. During that last year of her life, I never heard Gladys complaining about her sickness or the physical suffering she was subject to or the nights she could not sleep. Gladys died like a true woman, brave and loving as she had always been.

I believe that she kept being firm and brave because she knew that had I seen her crying or sad, I would suffer even more. She wanted me to remember her smiling, telling me how much she loved me, and how huge her love was for me. She was stronger than her suffering, thinking more of me than of her. She knew that her suffering would end before mine, and that is why she encouraged me to get on with my life.

To write these nine chapters have allowed me to meditate about this extraordinary woman's legacy, which I will attempt to describe in the final chapter.

# CHAPTER X -
# GLADYS MORALES' LEGACY

To define Gladys' legacy is a complex task because she had many virtues and touched many hearts.

According to the *Merriam Webster Dictionary* online, the simple definition of legacy is "a) *something (such as property or money) that is received from someone who has died: or b) as something happened in the past or that comes from someone in the past.*"

Consulting other sources (for example the Royal Academy of Spain), legacy is "*something that is transmitted to successors, be it material or immaterial.*"

Coincidentally, at the time I was writing this chapter, I received an email containing a link to a video called "What Will Matter" by Steve Polite, which refers to the concept of legacy. The link is https://player.vimeo.com/video/89476173. The components of this video, in my opinion, can be interpreted as components of a legacy. Here they are:

1. What you had given, what you had taught.

2. Your acts of integrity, compassion, or sacrifice, which had enriched and inspired others to emulate your example.

3. Your character.

4. The number of people who had mourned your loss.

5. The transparency and care with which you had loved other people, who had benefitted from you.

6. The memories that live and stay in the minds of the people you had loved.

7. The time that your memory lasts, in whom and for what reason.

As an exceptional witness of Gladys' life, I can say—without any doubt—that her legacy can be measured by each and every one of the preceding components.

A concrete way to feel my wife's legacy was a celebratory mass in her honor, held in our church St. Paul's-by-the-Lake in Chicago on Sunday, October 18, 2015, twelve days after she passed away. On that memorable day, I saw Gladys' impact through the attendance of my colleagues at DePaul's University (seventeen faculty members with their spouses), students, brothers and sisters in faith at the church, my friends, including a family who came from Rockford to Chicago, the director of The Selfhelp Home in which my wife died, and one of the managers of La Posada, where we stayed for five months in 1996 shortly after arriving in the United States from Mexico.

At the end of the mass, three persons summarized the impact she had on their lives. Just before finishing the activity, I dedicated a song to Gladys, which represented our love relationship since its very beginning in 1975.

The church was almost full. At the altar, there were four objects: Gladys' remains in a small brown box, a vase with flowers sent by my colleagues, a photo of our marriage ceremony in Havana—in which I was hugging her with a smile on my face and glittering eyes expressing satisfaction—and a photo taken thirty-five years later in Chicago, in which I was seated and she was standing behind me placing her two hands on my shoulders denoting protection. The comparison between the two photos represented my transformation from being a "*machista*" to a family man under Gladys' influence.

I was visibly emotional but simultaneously stable. I appeared to be calm and started to sing "Parla piu Piano." My voice sounded pleasant, representing the harmonious togetherness the couple had held during four decades. As I was approaching the end of the song, my voice sounded louder and the coda was sung with a very high tone that sounded like thunder in the church. The final words of the song stated that there could not be a love greater than ours.

For a moment, I remained silent as if I had received external support from Gladys. After the ceremony, everybody went to the second floor of the church to talk about Gladys' life.

As part of the legacy, I must also say that she was a human being with virtues and shortcomings. My wife recognized her own limitations and helped me discover mine. My wife oftentimes emphasized that she had always loved me regardless of my deficiencies.

In a snapshot, then, what is my own definition of Gladys's legacy? I think that it was to spread love in all its dimensions: for her partner, family, co-workers, students, instructors, brothers and sisters in faith at the church, the children, the elderly, and especially those who were in the lower social strata, for whom she felt compassion and respect. In the first place, though, I must mention her adoration for God, which Gladys transmitted through daily behavior in whatever circumstance, even when she could not boldly express it during our period in Cuba's Castro-Communism. My wife's human relations were outstanding and impacted everybody's conscience.

A few days after her death – as part of paying homage to her life – I offered three song-concerts to the residents of The Selfhelp Home – the nursing home where she died, and was so well looked after. One student-photographer took a photo of mine while I was singing and managed to combine it with one of Gladys'. In this special photo

Gladys is represented as if she were a ghost, her hands placed on my shoulder in a protective way.

As a final advice to my readers, I invite them to follow Gladys' example of love, modesty, dignity, bravery, sincerity, kindness and joy of living. Enjoy love and show it with actions and words to all your loved ones. Keep telling them how much you care. You will feel much better, and have a great internal peace that will help you mitigate the grief at the time of losing one of them.

Antonio E. Morales-Pita

# SURVEY

The author has created a brief survey to enable the reader to measure his/her progress in achieving a successful love relationship before and after reading this book. In the table below, it is only necessary to check the cell – that best matches your situation at the moment of filling in the table – with an "X".

If the first ten questions are answered "always" or "frequently" the reader is expected to be a member of a happy couple, or at least in the way to be so.

If the last five questions (11 through 15) are answered "always" or "frequently" the reader should be facing problems with the partner, but it might be possible to solve them if he/she tries to do so.

Forty years ago when I met Gladys, my answers to the first ten questions were located in either "seldom" or "never;" and to the last five questions, in either "always" or "frequently." After Gladys passed away I can affirm that – thanks to her patience and love – my answers to the first ten questions were located either "always" or "frequently;" while my last questions, in either "seldom" or "never."

The author recommends the readers to fill above table on several occasions: 1- Before reading the book; 2- After finishing the book; 3- one month after reading the book; 4- some months after reading the book.

The first step to solve a problem is to be aware of its existence, the second step is to interiorize the solution, and the third step is to make the decision to change for the better. This book intends to help the reader in achieving a successful love relationship.

| Question | Your answer | | | | |
|---|---|---|---|---|---|
| In relation my partner, I | Always | Fre-quently | Regularly | Seldom | Never |
| 1. express my love with words. | | | | | |
| 2. express my love with actions. | | | | | |
| 3. feel well when I get at home. | | | | | |
| 4. respect him/her and so I let him/her know with words and actions. | | | | | |
| 5. speak openly and clearly to him/her. | | | | | |
| 6. am proud of him/her and I let him/her know. | | | | | |
| 7. share domestic chores with him/her | | | | | |
| 8. support his/her aspirations. | | | | | |
| 9. support him/her sentimentally. | | | | | |
| 10. pay attention to his/her points of view | | | | | |
| 11. feel jealous and I let him/her know. | | | | | |
| 12. am in disagreement with him/her. | | | | | |
| 13. try to win all arguments. | | | | | |
| 14. compel him/her to do some-thing which he/she longs to. | | | | | |
| 15. impose my criterion on him/her. | | | | | |

# REVIEWS

"Many people ask themselves whether real love in fact does exist. Their answers are directly related to each individual's experience. The lucky ones — who had felt this wonderful feeling — would say yes, others experiencing *heart break after heart break* would say no, and there may be others who are waiting for, and dream about, a blissful loving experience.

In the book *Gladys, My Unforgettable Love*, Dr. Morales-Pita makes us feel what real love means. Citing his own words "to love and to be loved is a big human achievement." This achievement entails an authentic commitment. "In this same world full of wars, miseries, terrorist threats, hatred, and conflict, there is also tenderness. We have to discover this wonderful feeling in ourselves, our families, and our friends and to enjoy it as long as there is life. It would be a good way to comfort us in times of grief."

I invite everyone to read the story of a deep loving experience lasting forty years, six months and one day until death separated the couple. This is a deserved tribute to the woman who inspired this book. The author — through his narrative — transcends an example of a man, who honestly reveals his thoughts, feelings, and total transformation under the influence of his extraordinary wife. "

Mr. Raisa Mendoza, author and outstanding Hispanic lawyer, who has intensely worked in Chicago for nine years for the program Gift of Hope Chicago – a non for profit organization related to organ donation. She has also worked for Univision Radio, Radio Vive,

Mujeres sin Censura with Vicente Serrano as well as for Univision Telemundo, Mundo Fox and Cable 25.

"This book deals with the story of an outstanding woman, whose legacy is an example of love, compromise, and – above all – moral values."

Myrna Fragoso, President and Founder of Frida Kahlo Community Organization

Printed in Canada